Guide to the Collections

Museum of Grenoble

Guide to the Collections

by
Marianne Le Pommeré,
Laurent Salomé
and Christine Poullain
Translated by Bernard Hœpffner

Museum of Grenoble

Réunion
des Musées
Nationaux

ISBN 2 7118 3149 3
GK 39 3149

© Réunion des musées nationaux / Musée de Grenoble,
Paris, 1994
© Spadem, 1994
© ADAGP, 1994
© Succession H. Matisse, 1994

Acknowledgements

Our thanks are due to the authors of the detailed catalogues covering the collections of the Museum of Grenoble, and especially Catherine Chevillot, Marco Chiarini, Gilles Chomer and Marcel Destot, as well as Élizabeth Besson and Hélène Vincent, curators at the Museum of Grenoble, and Jeanine Scaringella, who supervised the editing work with her usual dedication and efficiency, and Isabelle Varloteaux, who put together the iconography.

Our thanks also go to all those who took an active part in the design and elaboration of the new display of the Museum of Grenoble:
The scientific staff: Laurent Salomé, Hélène Vincent, Danielle Bal, Élisabeth Besson, Christine Poullain, Isabelle Varloteaux.
The administrative staff: Françoise Merle, Denise Chafino, Maxence Girard, France Guillot, Michèle Revollon.
The library staff: Laurence Zeiliger, Nadine Vachier, Gérard Ponson.
The cultural department: Denis Arino, Marie-Josée Bourriot, Dany Philippe, Élisabeth de Rotalier, Claudine Sallenave, Marc Veyrat.
The technical staff: Jean-Louis Cristofol, Alain Argoud, André Carrel, Franck Chaize, Jacques Issartel, Philippe Dazey, Patrick Pauzin, Than N'Guyen, Patrice Rosset.
The secretarial staff: Jeanine Scaringella, Sandrine Lachaud, Nathalie Roche, Nicole Bouvier.
The reception staff: Marie-France Charles-Bernard, Marie-Dominique Argoud, Michèle Gaudu, Arlette Adnot.
The temporary staff: Isabelle Blachon, Pascal Boissin, Sophie Boubert, Cécile Brilloit, Jo Derval, Nadège Gaige, Sylvain Hanriot, Valérie Lagier, Emmanuelle Lefèvre, Édouard Du Masle, Serge Martel, Marie-Ange Millière, Bertrand Pauty, Xavier Pommaret, Jean-Paul Rozand, Christophe Terpent.
as well as the technical department of the City of Grenoble.

Finally, our thanks go to the restorers who, under the direction
of France Dijoud of the restoration department of Musées de France,
saw the work through to completion: Jeanne Amoore, Jean-François Bardez,
Georges-Louis Barthe, Nathalie et Aloÿs de Becdelièvre, Claire Bergeaud,
Jacques Bionner, Maria Bohusz, Laurence Calegagri, Anne-Carole Chaumard,
David Cueco, Régina da Costa Pinto Moreira, Bernard Delaval, Florence Delteil,
Emmanuel Desroches, Cécile Dubruel, Madeleine Fabre, Florence Half-Wrobel,
Catherine Haviland, Franziska et Jacques Hourrière, Jean-François Hulot,
Alain Jarry, Michel Jeanne, Carole Juillet, Pascale Klein, Lionel Lefevre,
Robert Mallet, Patrick Mandron, Hervé Manis, Christine Mouterde,
Anthony Pontabry, Thérèse Prunet, Marie-France Racine, Alain Roche,
Jacqueline Roussel, Marie-Rosa Sreca, Véronique Stedman, Serge Thiers,
Colette Vicat-Blanc, Monsieur et Madame Wade-Leegenboek.

Table of contents	Foreword by Serge Lemoine	9
Rooms 58 to 60	Antiquities by Marianne Le Pommeré	13
Rooms 1 to 24	Ancient Art by Marianne Le Pommeré	17
Rooms 1 to 10	13th to 17th Century Works	18
Rooms 11 to 14	18th Century Works	61
Rooms 15 to 24	19th Century Works	74
Rooms 25 to 53	20th Century Art by Marianne Le Pommeré	97
Tour de l'Isle	Drawings Collection	202
	Ancient Drawings by Laurent Salomé	203
	Modern Drawings by Christine Poullain	218
	Selective Bibliography	239
	Index of works reproduced, by artists' names	241

View of the museum, Place de Lavalette.

Foreword

The Museum of Grenoble, the most important French museum of modern art outside Paris, has the good fortune also to own an exceptional collection of paintings, sculptures and drawings dating from the Renaissance to the end of the 19th century, as well as a celebrated collection of ancient Egyptian art. The collections, which could not be displayed entirely in the original building, have now been divided up among the rooms of the new museum, which was designed by three young architects from Grenoble — Antoine Félix-Faure, Olivier Félix-Faure and Philippe Macary — with the help of Lorenzo Piqueras for specifically museographical matters; it is intended to accommodate the collections under the best conditions of conservation, and to show them off to their best advantage. The museum was inaugurated in 1994. The works of art are displayed according to a certain number of historical, artistic and museological principles, and, to begin with, in chronological order: this brings out the evolution of ideas over time, the differences between schools — to the extent that this term still makes sense — and the nature of the various movements, such as Impressionism or Cubism. The works are also displayed according to other principles, e.g. their size (large formats are set apart from small easel paintings), their technique (two of the rooms contain only sculptures), and the artists (Philippe de Champaigne's painting are shown together). The works are sometimes organized by genre (landscapes, portraits, etc.). This layout has also been used, *mutatis mutandis*, for contemporary works, which are well represented in the museum's collections, and this has made it possible to organize the presentation of the works according to period and artistic principles, thus allowing the viewer to make meaningful comparisons and links.

A few words of explanation should be given as regards the works themselves, as well as their form, technique and meaning, if they are to be enjoyed fully. Hence this guide, whose aim is to give an explanation and to facilitate the appreciation of the extraordinary variety of Western artistic creation that is present in the Museum of Grenoble's collections.

This variety should not come as a surprise. The museum, founded in 1796 by Louis-Joseph Jay, long before any other French provincial museum, was immediately able to acquire works of great quality, while at the same time being entrusted by the State with remarkable works. Throughout the 19th century, the collection was enriched yet again by judicious acquisitions (works by Canaletto and Delacroix), and by particularly large donations, such as that of Léonce Mesnard, which became the nucleus of the drawings collection, and that of General de Beylié, who gave the museum, among other works, four paintings by Zurbarán, which are still admired by visitors from all over the world. At the beginning of the 20th century, the collection of ancient art had more or less attained its present form: most of the great artists, as well as all the schools — French, Italian, Spanish, Flemish and Dutch — and artistic currents from Mannerism to the School of Barbizon, from Caravaggism to Baroque art, not forgetting Ancient Egypt, and indeed all the particular genres, from the still life to the allegory, as well as historical paintings, portraits and religious compositions. In other words all the disciplines, from oil painting to prints, drawing and sculpture included, are represented at the Museum of Grenoble.

In 1919, Andry-Farcy (1882-1950) was appointed director of this prestigious institution, and occupied the post until 1949. He was interested in modern art, and in thirty years built up a collection in which all the artistic tendencies of the first half of the century were represented, from Fauvism to Abstraction, from Cubism to naïve painting; he also acquired comprehensive bodies of work, such as Belgian art, where Expressionism (Permeke), Abstraction (Servranckx) and Surrealism (Magritte) can be found. The same policy was followed by his successors, and the 20th century collection of the museum is the foremost in France, if one excepts the Musée National d'Art Moderne in Paris. A great number of works have no equivalent in French public collections, or were the first of a particular artist to be acquired. In sum, a very large number of artists of all tendencies are represented — the collection cannot, however, be said to be a mere sample. The whole

19th century sculpture room.

20th century art room.

collection is exceptional, and its value rivals that of the most important European museums. Henceforth housed in a new building covering a total area of 18,000 m^2, it satisfies modern needs and requirements in terms of museography and public facilities. In this new building — which also contains a specialized library, an auditorium, conference rooms, a workshop for children, a cafeteria and a bookshop — sixty-five rooms are open to the public and 1,500 works are on permanent display in an area of 6,000 m^2. There is no other structure of this type in France.

It was thus deemed necessary to provide a guide for visitors. Marianne Le Pommeré has written the texts for the paintings and sculptures, from the Middle Ages to the present day, as well as for the Antiquities; for this she used the available scientific works which analyze the Grenoble collection, published on the occasion of the museum's opening, and listed at the end of this guide. Marianne Le Pommeré's intention was to express, in a clear and concise style, the main characteristics of the works as they are presented in the various rooms. As concerns ancient and modern drawings, Christine Poullain and Laurent Salomé decided to make a selection from a collection which is still largely unknown, and which contains some surprising items. And the overall aim of the guide is to give visitors the information they need on the works in the Museum of Grenoble's collections, which are now at last properly displayed, room after room, work after work; it is hoped that a visit will thus be as illuminating as it is pleasant, and that our visitors will be encouraged to go further with their discoveries.

Serge Lemoine

Antiquities

Rooms 58 to 60

Unless otherwise stated, measurements are given in centimetres.

Sarcophagus of Psammetk

Saite-Persian era, *c.* 500 B.C.
Stuccoed and painted wood
185 x 133
Gift of Saint-Ferriol, 1916

This sarcophagus, pictorially the most beautiful example in the Museum of Grenoble, consists of a trough and lid hollowed out from a single block. It represents a mummy wrapped in its linen winding-sheet; the head is covered with a wig whose stylized locks, which are black and yellow, pass round the back of the figure, framing a face painted green, with black eyes and a long beard turned up at the end. The frontal decoration is divided into two zones: the upper part, corresponding to the shoulders and torso, forms an elaborately ornamented pattern above the representation of three goddesses; the lower part — the legs — is comprised of hieroglyphic signs making up traditional texts, within parallel vertical bands. The back features two further columns of text. The whole is in a good state of preservation, and was painstakingly executed. The figures and hieroglyphs were painted with great finesse and the colours have been particularly well harmonized. Each one of the figured elements has an astounding pictorial quality.

Goddess Giving the Sign of Life to the King

Wall fragment from
the temple of Karnak-North
Reign of Nectanebo II (360-343 B.C.)
Yellow sandstone
76 x 66
Gift of Saint-Ferriol, 1916

This relief comes from the shrine of the high temple of Karnak-North, and represents a goddess giving the sign of life to the king. The two are standing, face to face, their clothing and accessories are typical of the period, and their postures are finely observed. This fragment, which is now shown as a work on its own, is a sculpture of great quality, with firm, supple lines and clearly delineated volumes; and this has been achieved without any loss of realism.

Funeral Stela

Athens, 1st century B.C.
Pentelic marble
181 x 102 x 32
Entered in 1796

This funeral stela, which dates from the 1st century B.C., was given to the public library of Grenoble in 1788 by Joseph de Flotte, who had brought it from Greece in 1782. And when the Museum of Grenoble was inaugurated, it naturally found a place there. The piece, in a very good state of preservation, bears the signature of "Aristokles", a sculptor from Rhodes, and is extremely rare. It represents a man and a woman, in three-quarters profile, standing under an arcature resting on two pilasters. The woman is touching the man's chin in a gesture which, in antiquity, was a sign of welcome. The elaborate folds, the precise forms, and the relation between the figures and the frame — these are clear demonstrations of the masterful technique of the sculptor, who has successfully drawn upon the classical tradition without perverting it.

Ancient Art   17

Rooms 1 to 24

13TH TO 17TH CENTURY WORKS

rooms 1 to 10

18 Jacopo Torriti (attrib.)

Active in Rome (Italy), 1287 to 1292

Ancient Art

Saint Lucy

Tempera on wood
170 x 64
Gift of General de Beylié, 1901

This is the museum's oldest Italian painting; it is most probably the central panel of a triptych which was commissioned by a lady, Angela Cerroni (shown in the lower part of the composition), after she had been cured of an eye ailment. Saint Lucy, on account of her name (i.e. *lux* = light), was often called upon by people suffering from diseases of the eyes. The painting — a major work in terms of its origin, rarity and state of preservation — is iconographically very interesting: it might be the oldest known representation of Saint Lucy "holding a lamp". Although the frontal treatment is archaic in style, the slight undulations in the folds of the cloak, and the way the angels have been painted, prefigure the immense mutations that Italian painting was to undergo at the start of the 14th century, especially in Giotto's work.

Taddeo di Bartolo

Siena (Italy), *c.* 1362 — 1422

Virgin and Child between Saint Gerard, Saint Paul, Saint Andrew and Saint Nicholas

Tempera on wood
Central panel: 170 x 75
Lateral panels: 152 x 75
Loaned by the Louvre in 1876

This triptych, painted for the church of San Paolo all'Orto, in Pisa, is reminiscent of the cross-section of a church. It is one of the finest primitivist works in the museum's possession, and although the predella, corner pillars and pinnacles are missing, it has retained its majestic quality. In this representation of the Virgin in Majesty, Taddeo di Bartolo has for the first time replaced the Virgin's throne, or cushion, by a seraphim motif. The child, shown standing on his mother's knee, has a finger in the beak of a goldfinch, as a symbol of the soul drinking the Eucharistic blood that will save it. Saint Paul, the patron saint of the church of San Paolo all'Orto who can be recognized by his sword, as well as by the letter he is holding on which are written the words "Ad Romanos", stands to the right of the Virgin; beside him is Gerard de Villamagna, in Franciscan robes, holding a rosary; above them, in a medallion, is Saint Gregory, who is shown writing under the inspiration of the Holy Spirit, represented as a dove. To the left of the Virgin is Saint Andrew, holding a book and a cross, with Saint Nicholas, bishop of Myra, carrying the three gold balls of the legend and, finally, in a medallion, Saint Louis, in a robe patterned with fleurs-de-lys, holding the attributes of royalty. This triptych is remarkably executed, especially the gilded parts, and is one of the finest examples of the technique used by the Sienese master, despite the awkward rendering of the hands and feet.

Saint Sebastian and Saint Apollonia

Il Perugino (Pietro Vannuci)

Città della Pieve (Italy), *c.* 1450
Fontignano (Italy), 1523

Tempera on wood
189 x 95
Presented by the State, 1811

This panel was part of a two-sided polyptych in the shape of a Roman triumphal arch made up of fifteen panels with a predella; its place was at the loft of the central panel, which illustrated the Nativity. From 1495 until his death in 1523 Perugino worked on this altarpiece, which was divided up in the 17th century. The two saints represented are Saint Sebastian and Saint Apollonia, the latter with a book and a pair of pincers holding a tooth, the symbol of her martyrdom.

As this panel was left unfinished — there is no glaze on Saint Apollonia's cloak, nor on the feet of either figure — it may be assumed that the work was painted towards the end of the artist's life. The high pictorial quality of the work suggest that it was painted by Perugino himself, unlike the other panels, whose execution was mainly left to his students.

Cesare da Sesto (attrib.)

Sesto Calende (Italy), 1477
Milan (Italy), 1523

Christ Carrying His Cross

Oil on wood
65 x 79
Presented by the State, 1811

This is a characteristic painting of the 16th century Milanese school. The composition is remarkable for the simple, bold geometry used to highlight the narrative: the overpowering diagonal of the cross, heightened by the position of the head of Mary Magdalene who is holding the Virgin's body, marks a boundary between the world of light and the world of darkness; in a similar way, the crosspiece is accentuated by the diagonal in the corner formed by the unconscious body of the Virgin. The rich palette and the delicacy of the chiaroscuro technique, which is applied with great mastery, derive from Leonardo da Vinci and Raphael; the movement of the eyes and hands is of great dramatic quality.

This work has been attributed with a degree of certainty to Cesare da Sesto, who often foreshortened figures in a similar way to what is found here in the depiction of Mary Magdalene's head.

Christ Meeting the Wife and Sons of Zebedee

Oil on canvas
194 x 337
Presented by the State, 1811

Veronese (Paolo Caliari)

Verona (Italy), 1528
Venice (Italy), 1588

This painting illustrates a Biblical episode in which Zebedee's widow asks Christ that her sons James and John may be permitted to sit by his side in his Kingdom, to the surprise and indignation of the other apostles. James "the Greater" and John "the Evangelist" were the last to be chosen as apostles by Christ.

The composition is that of a frieze, with an opposition between two areas of equal size: Christ and five apostles are shown against an architectural background, while Zebedee's widow, along with James and John, is shown against a background of sky. The monumental character of the painting is due to the size of the figures, which take up almost the whole height of the canvas, as well as to the verticality of the bodies, which are clothed in the three primary colours of their flowing robes, and the powerful antique columns. The proportions of the verticals are masterfully counterbalanced by the broken line formed by the arms and hands of the figures. Christ, who is shown to the left of the centre, is framed by the two columns and he is thrown into relief by the play of the light. The simple, stark composition of this painting, the clarity of the narrative, and the quality of the execution, notably in the heads of the figures — veritable portraits, in fact — indicate that it is one of Veronese's major works, which was, at one time, in the collection of Louis XIV.

Giorgio Vasari

Arezzo (Italy), 1511
Florence (Italy), 1574

The Holy Family

Oil on wood
177 x 136
Presented by the State, 1811

This work is characteristic of the Mannerist school that was prevalent in Italy from 1527 onwards, as is particularly clear from the opaque, closed space, the convoluted curves and counter-curves of the unnatural folds in the garments, the complex postures, the monumental proportions of the bodies, and the complex overall geometry of the composition. The Holy Family had never been represented in this way, with Joseph and Saint Anne in prominent positions, and the Infant Jesus shown sleeping; without a halo, he is is no longer a newborn baby, but an ordinary child, with nothing divine about him. The direction of the light adds to the strangeness of the composition: it is focused on the centre, and has the effect of bleaching the colours. A number of erudite references can be deciphered: the monumental treatment of the Virgin, as well as the position of her arms and that of Jesus' body, is reminiscent of certain works by Michelangelo and Raphael. The very high quality of the work indicates that it was entirely executed by Vasari.

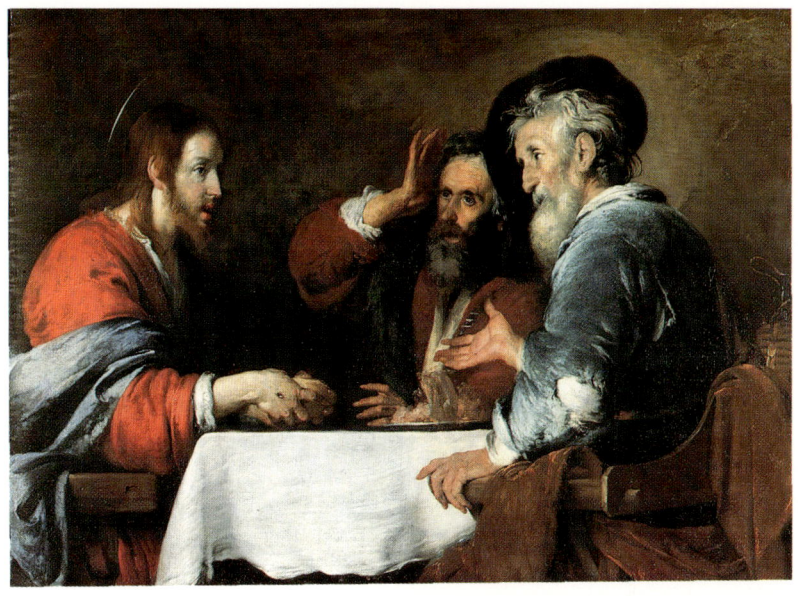

Christ at Emmaus

Oil on canvas
124 x 172
Presented by the State, 1811

Bernardo Strozzi

Genoa (Italy), 1581
Venice (Italy), 1644

This painting represents Christ, who is in the act of breaking bread, being recognized by the two disciples at Emmaus. The figures are shown in half-length from close at hand, which enables the viewer to enter easily into the intimacy of the scene; the three portraits presented here are of great psychological finesse. The brushstrokes are nervous and full, the colours are bright, and a few revealing details, such as the blue robe with silver tones worn by the disciple on the right, suggest that the painting dates from Strozzi's Venetian period, at the height of his maturity, when he had perfectly assimilated the lessons of Caravaggio's art, and applied them to his own work.

Mattia Preti, known as Il Calabrese

The Martyrdom of Saint Peter

Taverna (Italy), 1613
Malta, 1699

Oil on canvas
335 x 242
Acquired in 1828

The provenance and original location of this painting, which depicts the martyrdom of Saint Peter, are unknown. The scene is captured at the point of maximum intensity, in a penumbra traversed by slashes of light — a pictorial equivalent of violence and suffering. In a space with no recognizable planes, the baroque composition organizes the volumes along two diagonals that intersect on Saint Peter's torso; the masses, which appear too dense to be contained within the overdrawn vertical rectangle of the support, add to the pictorial expression of violence. The dramatic and constructive luminism, and the realistic rendering of violence, show that Preti was acquainted with Caravaggio's technique, which he probably acquired while he was a student of Battistello, the most remarkable of Caravaggio's disciples. Such characteristics would tend to suggest that this work was painted during the Roman period (between 1630 and 1650) of Preti's long and prolific career.

Martyrdom of Saint Catherine   **Caspar de Crayer**

Oil on canvas
242 x 188
Presented by the State, 1811

Antwerp (Antwerp), 1584
Ghent (Flanders), 1669

This masterpiece, which belongs to the museum's Flemish collection, represents Saint Catherine at the moment when, by order of the emperor Maxentius, having survived being tortured on the spiked wheel, she is about to be beheaded before the statue of the pagan god she had refused to worship. The composition, which is solidly constructed along two diagonals, is of a monumental character, enhanced by the fact that the figures are arranged in tiers, and by the direction of the eyes: thus the executioner, standing above the saint on the last step, and whose body is shown in its entirety against the pale sky, appears to loom over the viewer. The painting was commissioned in 1622 by a surgeon of Courtrai for the chapel of one of the town's churches; it is a paean to Saint Catherine in the spirit of the Counter-Reformation, and was intended to inspire a revival in the worship of the saints and the Virgin. The scene of Saint Catherine's martyrdom betrays no suffering — the faces are calm, the bodies young and beautiful. The dominant colours are blue and red, with rare modulations (e.g. the bluish grey of the horse), and vibrate to the dissonant purple colour of the saint's dress. These sumptuous colours, and the movement which runs through the work, make it one of de Crayer's finest paintings.

Peter Paul Rubens

Siegen (Westphalia), 1577
Antwerp (Antwerp), 1640

*Saint Gregory, Pope,
Surrounded by Saints*

1606-1607
Oil on canvas
477 x 288
Presented by the State, 1811

This is the most significant work in the museum's Flemish collection. Rubens had been commissioned by the Oratorian Brothers to provide a painting for the main altar of their new church, dedicated to Saint Maria de Vallicella, which had been donated to them in 1575 by Pope Gregory XIII.

The figures represented are: in the centre of the composition, Gregory I, pope from 590 to 604, patron saint of the Church; to the right, Saint Domitilla, Saint Achilleus and Saint Nereus, whose relics were kept in the church; to the left, Saint Maurice — a figure borrowed by Rubens from Correggio's *Madonna with Saint George* (Dresden, Gemäldegalerie) — wearing a Roman soldier's breastplate; and, behind him, Saint Papianus, leaning on a long staff. This gathering of saints is placed under an antique triumphal arch bearing an image of the Madonna and Child conferring blessings, surrounded by cherubs.

It would appear that it was only when Rubens did a second version of the picture that he introduced the particular representation of the Virgin Mary seen here: he had been asked to use the image of the Virgin Mary, as painted by Saint Luke, that was thought to have accomplished the miracle of dispelling pestilential miasmas during the pontificate of Gregory I. The new church altar was finally presented with a copy of the Grenoble painting, for Rubens, who in his correspondence commends "the exquisite quality of colouring, the subtlety of the heads and materials reproduced from nature", thought the lighting conditions in the church deplorable; he later reworked the piece, and, in 1626, placed it in the Antwerp chapel where his mother and first wife were buried. In 1800, it was taken from the chapel by French troops.

The monumental character of this work, in which space appears to have no recognizable planes, and to be bursting with huge figures organized along diagonal lines and dressed in splendid costumes with large folds, along with the spacious, airy pictorial treatment, the surprising dialogue of Saint Papianus and Saint Domitilla with the viewer, and the theatrical postures — these elements form the basis of a new language. Rubens, in the first period of his career, having already spent some years studying the Venetian colorists and the sense of architecture of the Mannerists, was inventing the Baroque aspects of his art.

Jacob Jordaens

Antwerp (Antwerp), 1593-1678

The Adoration of the Shepherds

Oil on canvas
255 x 175
Presented by the State, 1803

The exuberance of this large composition, where each figure is a pretext for the invention of an anecdote as well as the object of a careful study (the pretty hand holding the lion cub on a leash, the dazzled man, etc.), indicate that this is one of Jordaens' early work. And indeed, though he was only twenty-four when he finished the painting, it displays the main characteristics of his art. It appears to draw its inspiration directly from a painting done by Rubens on the same subject, in 1617-1619, for the triptych of Saint Jean de Malines (coll. of the Museum of Marseille). Jordaens was more than a student of Rubens, and in fact worked for twenty years as his collaborator. The influences exerted by Caravaggio — his sense of reality and of the lighting effects — and by Correggio — from whom Jordaens borrowed the ideas of the cherubs on a cloud, the shepherd dazzled by light, and the standing shepherd holding a lantern — are also manifest here. Having studiously assimilated these influences, Jordaens constructed a powerful image with bold foreshortenings, and treated all his figures with the same care, in a clear intimation of his Baroque tendencies and the generosity of his outlook.

God Chastising Adam and Eve

c. 1623-1625
Oil on copper
95 x 75
Loaned by the State in 1892

Domenichino
(Domenico Zampieri)

Bologna (Italy), 1581
Naples (Italy), 1641

This beautiful painting was presented to Louis XIV by Charles Le Nôtre in 1693. The complex representation is extremely faithful to the Biblical iconography that had so often been used in the Middle Ages: thus, the tree on the left is a fig tree and not an apple tree, and Adam and Eve wear girdles made from the leaves of that tree. God the Father, wrapped in the folds of a large floating mantle and surrounded by angels, is directly inspired by the figure of God the Father as represented by Michelangelo in his *Creation of Man*, but the animals scattered over the landscape are weird and wonderful: the sheep and the lion (which also appear in the other two versions of this painting) are a symbol of peaceful coexistence (the same notion also being expressed in the background, where a stag, a hound, a bear and a heron are found gathered together), while the horse is an indication of emergent sensuality. The addition of two angels and three cherubim above God's cloak conforms to the Biblical text. The particularly fine pictorial treatment of this work, the bright, deep colours, the careful representation of the landscape, all of these things reveal Domenichino's interest in Northern painting, and his probable knowledge of painters such as Jan "Velvet" Brueghel.

Abraham Bloemaert

Gorinchem (Netherlands), 1564
Utrecht (Netherlands), 1651

Adoration of the Magi

1623
Oil on canvas
424 x 290
Loaned by the State in 1811

Painted for the high altar of the new Jesuit church in Brussels, the *Adoration of the Magi* is the most important work by this Dutch painter to be found in a French public collection. Bloemaert's fidelity to the European Mannerist style, of which he was the leading figure in Utrecht, can clearly be seen in this picture, which was painted during the last years of the artist's life.

Bloemaert set his scene in the open air, heightening his colours by introducing acid tones (some of the clothes appearing as patches of green) and dissonances (as can be seen in the relations between the colours in the cloak of the Magus who is offering his gift in the foreground). The elongated figures, their postures, and the extreme luxury and refinement of their costumes, belong to the canons of beauty and elegance elaborated by the Mannerists. These features are accentuated with subtlety by a composition in tiers stretching up towards the vertical, as well as by the contrast between the two zones and the distortion in the scale of the figures, which are huge in the foreground and small in the middle ground. The bold diagonals that structure the scene, and the formal exuberance of colouring, show to what extent Baroque art was steeped in Mannerism.

John the Baptist Preaching

c. 1600
Oil on canvas
39 x 52
Loaned by the State in 1897

Annibale Carracci

Bologna (Italy), 1560
Rome (Italy), 1609

This small painting was at one time in the collection of Cardinal Mazarin, then that of Cardinal Richelieu, who sold it to Louis XIV in 1665. It is an important example of the mastery attained by Annibale Carracci in the art of landscape painting.

The balanced order of successive planes, the groups of figures, whose distribution creates an effect of depth, and the detailed rendering of vegetation and rocks — all these elements come together to create an idealized landscape. It was with such works that Annibale Carracci laid the foundations of Roman Classicism, which remained a model for painters until the 19th century.

Francesco Albani

Bologna (Italy), 1578-1660

The Holy Family in a Landscape

Oil on copper
34 x 43
Presented by the State, 1811

The Madonna and the Infant sleeping in her lap are being contemplated by Saint Joseph, who is sitting beside them on a wooden bench, an open book in one hand, his head resting on the other. Two angels can be seen in adoration on the left, and three cherubim hover above the central group. In the background, a forest of trees and bushes merges on the right with a river landscape featuring a bridge and a small waterfall.

The colours are typical of Albani's style during the last years of his life: a red dress and blue cloak for the Virgin, a dark yellow cloak and purple robe for Saint Joseph, white and yellow robes for the two angels.

Albani settled in Bologna in 1617 after spending sixteen years in Rome, where he was Annibale Carracci's assistant in the decoration of the Galleria of the Palazzio Farnese; he was a successful painter, and pursued a prolific career up until his death, at a very advanced age. During the Bologna period, and especially after 1630, great quantities of routine work came out of his studio, most often produced by his assistants. It was at this time that Albani painted a series of small intimist works for a private clientele; these were often done on copper, in an oval format: the Grenoble painting belongs to this body of later work.

Here the theme of the Holy Family is only a pretext for the landscape. The boat on the far right might be an indication that the painter had in mind the episode of the Return of the Holy Family.

Cavalry Battle

Oil on canvas
51 x 75
Gift of Mme Casimir Périer, 1839

Michelangelo Cerquozzi, known as Michelangelo of the Battles

Rome (Italy), 1602-1660

Although Cerquozzi produced a great number of battle scenes — which gave him his name — his artistic personality has still not been defined.

This painting is rare in that it represents the scene of a battle between Turks and Christians. The standard displayed here bears the arms of the Medici, and the work may have been destined for Florence. The central group, where the figures are strongly contrasted by the use of chiaroscuro, stands out against the luminous sky and is painted in great detail. It should be noted that Cerquozzi belonged to the Roman circle of the "Bamboccianti", artists grouped around the Dutch painter Pieter van Laer, called Il Bamboccio, who liked painting genre pictures requiring carefully worked details and a sense of anecdote.

Ancient Art

Osias Beert

Flowers, Fruit, Vases and Other Objects

Antwerp (Antwerp), *c.* 1580-1624

Oil on wood
52 x 73
Acquired in 1798

This painting is part of a set of four still lifes, attributed to Osias Beert, which are to be found in the Flemish collection of the Museum of Grenoble; Beert was one of the most important Flemish painters of still lifes. The composition, similar to that of *Vegetables, Fruits and Cups*, is centered on a bunch of tulips and is in a state of apparent disorder: the composition is seen from a raised perspective and the objects are viewed in their entirety, arranged in two oblique lines, and the support appears to merge with the table on which they are placed. Tulips were highly sought-after at the time, and collectors paid huge sums of money for them. The tripod egg-cup and the knife with the chequered handle — also objects of luxury — indicate the pursuit of beauty. The other elements have a moral connotation: the fallen petals, and also the fragile dragonfly, are there to express the vanity of all things.

The moral lesson is extremely discreet, and what finally comes through is the pleasure of a painter fascinated by riches and beauty.

Card Game at an Inn

Oil on wood
62 x 87
Loaned by the Louvre in 1937

David Teniers, the Younger

Antwerp (Antwerp), 1610
Brussels (Brabant), 1690

The virtuosity of David Teniers the Younger brought him immense success, and he had a prolific career. He was at home with all genres, and most especially with scenes of daily life, in which he was influenced by the art of Adriaen Brouwer. *Card Game at an Inn*, which can be dated 1640-45, is organized according to a plan often used by the artist: an L-shaped room on two levels. Two sources of light — a window and a half-open door — are used to divide the figures into two groups, the card players on the left and a group of women and children on the right. The moralizing symbolism of the broken pipes and the caged bird is improbable. And in fact, the painting, with its restricted range of greys and ochres, is an image whose slightly down-to-earth realism illustrates everyday life and peaceful harmony.

Frans Snyders

Parrots and Other Birds

Antwerp (Antwerp), 1579-1657

Oil on wood
122 x 98
Loaned by the State in 1811

Although Frans Snyders studied with Pieter Brueghel the Younger, it was in the art of Italy — where he lived for a year — and also in Rubens' work, that the main influences on his art are to be found. In this painting, various tropical birds, brought to Holland by Dutch ships, are shown perching on the branches of an apricot tree. The composition is resolutely Baroque: an open, yet overcrowded space, divided by diagonals, unstructured by planes. The undisguisedly monumental quality of this work and the palette of bright colours marked a new phase in the style of Snyders, who was a recognized master of genre paintings.

The Punishment of Callisto

Bartholomeus Breenbergh

Oil on canvas
37 x 48.7
Gift of Auguste Gérard, 1899

Deventer (Netherlands), *c.* 1599-1600
Amsterdam (Netherlands), before 1657

In this work, which he painted in Amsterdam, Breenbergh makes extensive use of the studies of landscapes and ruins that he had done while living in Rome, between 1620 and 1633. The composition is structured by the diagonal division of the surface into two zones: the distant background, steeped in a pale, pink light, is opposed to the darker foreground, where Diana and her maids are shown against the light. The work is typical of Breenbergh's delicate, precious manner, the detailed nature of the description being characteristic of the Dutch school. Recent research has shown that the subject is not, as was previously thought, Diana at her toilet, but the incident where she discovers Callisto's pregnancy and, as a punishment, changes her into a she-bear: this may explain the outstretched arm of the goddess, the forefinger pointing towards two doves in the sky, the surprise of the black maid, and the almost hostile look of Callisto, who is partly covered by a heavy brown animal skin. When looking at this small amateur painting, it is difficult to decide which is more delightful: the elegance of the mythological narrative, the delicacy of the landscape, the preciosity of the still life detail, showing the attributes of the huntress and her jewelcase, or the pyramid formed by Callisto, in a standing position, obstinately silent, by Diana, seen from the back, drawn out in a long arabesque, and by her three maids.

Herman van Swanevelt

Landscape, Vesperal Effect

Woerden, near Utrecht (Netherlands), c. 1600
Paris (?), 1655

1644
Oil on canvas
88 x 89
Bequest of Georges Marjolin, 1896

Closely related to Claude Lorrain, with whom he shared a house in Rome in 1627, van Swanevelt left his mark on the history of French painting by introducing the artists of Paris, whom he visited frequently, to the classic landscape form that he had elaborated in Italy with his companion. The landscape in the Museum of Grenoble is a remarkable example of the modern conception of this genre. The composition is orthogonal in structure, the surface being boldly divided down the middle. The dappled foliage is done in evenly-spaced brushstrokes. The cold light coming from the left, beautifully observed, touches the trunk of a tree with silver, before flooding the vale on the right, adding depth to the space and modulating the rich range of greens, which are heightened by the bright tones of the clothes. The luminism and depth, together with the balance of the composition, lead to an idealization of the landscape.

River Bank

1633
Oil on wood
61.5 x 105
Bequeathed in 1903

Salomon van Ruysdael

Naardem (Netherlands), 1600
Haarlem (Netherlands), 1670

Salomon van Ruysdael, like his more famous nephew, Jacob van Ruisdael (1628/9-1682), was particularly fond of painting landscapes. This work is a perfect example of his art, above all as concerns the subject: a few houses and a tracery of trees, reflected in the smooth waters of a river, but also with the rectangular, horizontal format, which, as in most of van Ruysdael's paintings, is organized in horizontal layers: water — light colours; houses and trees — dark colours; sky — light colours; the palette is not very contrasted, consisting of subtle shades of acid green, greyish green and brown. The foliage is modelled without details, in pointillist touches that perfectly express the fragile aspect of form rendered hazy by movement.

Matthias Stomer

Amesfoort (Netherlands), 1600
Sicily (?), after 1650

The Dinner at Emmaus

Oil on canvas
130 x 164
Acquired in 1826

Matthias Stomer was a Dutch painter who spent most of his life in Italy. His work remains little known today. He belongs to the family of Tenebrist painters, disciples of Caravaggio, who, following Gerrit Van Honthorst, dramatized their compositions by the use of chiaroscuro and candlelight. This was the technique used by Stomer in this representation of the dinner at Emmaus, where the scene is plunged in obscurity relieved by a sole candle. Christ and the two pilgrims form a rectangle that is homothetic to the canvas and stabilized by the verticality of the candle in the centre. The two diagonals, indicated by the positions of the dog and the servant, lead the eye towards the group, where all the light is concentrated. The stark geometry is an exaltation of the bold treatment of shadow and light. The light of the candle, in an effect which is totally different from that produced by Georges de La Tour, overexposes and emphasizes the expressions on the faces and the gestures of the hands.

One might compare this painting with the treatments and styles of Bernardo Strozzi and Laurent de La Hyre, in their illustration of the same subject.

Belshazzar's Feast

Oil on canvas
147 x 174
Loaned by the State in 1863

Bartholomäus Strobel
(attrib.)

Breslau (Silesia), 1591 — after 1650

Belshazzar's Feast illustrates an episode from the Old Testament in which the King of Babylon, during a great feast where the wine was served in vessels his father had taken from the temple in Jerusalem, saw a hand writing the words "Mene, Tekel, Upharsin", which the prophet Daniel translated as "numbered, weighed, divided" and interpreted as predicting the death of Belshazzar and the end of his kingdom. This episode has rarely been represented, though it was made famous by Rembrandt's magnificent picture, painted around 1635. The present work is attributed to a little-known artist, Bartholomäus Strobel, who studied in Breslau with his father, then spent some time in Danzig, where he frequented the courts of the King of Poland and the Prince of Saxony. The image he created to evoke the feast shows the influence of the Mannerists from Holland and Prague, and has affinities with that of Jacques Bellange of Nancy: there is the density of the image, crowded out with the elongated figures and contorted postures of a multitude of lords and ladies, as well as the liberties taken with space, the way the scene is brutally cut off at the edges of the painting and extended in the background by the open door of the pantry, and also the elaborate composition in two sections, curiously placed side by side, with the oblique of the table next to the verticality of the musicians' gallery. The complex technique resembles a kind of writing, with thick layers of paint, sweeping brushstrokes, calculated nonchalance and the use of gold powder. All those effects are intended to bring out the meaning of the representation: the vile pleasure of desecrators before their terrible comeuppance.

Gerbrand van den Eeckhout

Amsterdam (Netherlands), 1621-1674

Portrait of Jan Pietersz van den Eeckhout

1644
Oil on wood
76 x 57.5
Acquired in 1825

This beautiful portrait was admired by Rembrandt, van den Eeckhout's teacher and friend. It is thought to represent the painter's brother, a craft-jeweller. The viewer's attention is drawn to the fragility of the sitter, finely brought out by the technique: light glazes of a warm tone have been applied to the tired features of the face and the hands, which have been coarsened by age more than by work. This type of portrait often uses symbolism — represented here by the *trompe-l'œil* nail on the window ledge — of a kind that would give the painting the value of a *Vanitas*. A counterpart of this work exists: the *Portrait of Cornelia Dedel*, the mother-in-law of the painter. It is also dated 1644, and is to be found in a private collection.

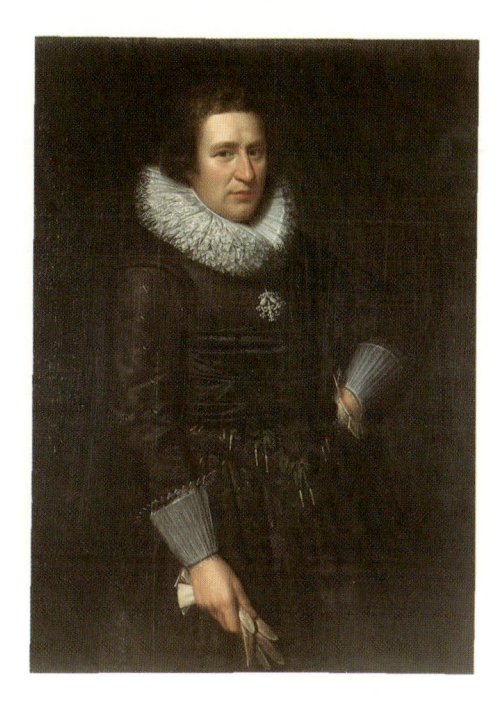

*Portrait
of a 21-Year-Old Man*

1619
Oil on wood
105 x 76
Bequest of Joseph Roman, 1926

**Nicolaes Eliasz,
"Pickenoy"** (attrib.)

Amsterdam (Netherlands),
1590 — *c.* 1653-1656

Pickenoy, who was one of the most highly appreciated painters in Amsterdam before Rembrandt's importance came to be recognized, is known mainly for a large group portrait, dated 1642, of *The Company of Captain Jan Claesz.* The painting in the Museum of Grenoble, today attributed to Pickenoy, illustrates the same art of portraiture. The setting is typical of his manner: on a plain, bare background, the model is shown in three-quarters profile, while the face, underlined by the white ruff, is turned towards the viewer. Though many of Pickenoy's portraits show this same slightly ironical expression, these same firm, intelligent eyes, he was strongly attached to painting the true character of his models. The smooth pictorial treatment exalts the beauty of the palette, in brilliant grey-blacks.

Claude Vignon

Tours, 1593
Paris, 1670

Jesus amongst the Doctors

1623
Oil on canvas
153 x 224
Presented by the State, 1811

This painting illustrates an episode from the New Testament with Jesus, at the age of twelve, "sitting in the midst of the doctors, both hearing them, and asking them questions. [...] And all that heard him were astonished at his understanding and answers." It was probably painted either in Rome, or in France, immediately after Vignon's return. The bare background, enlivened by a ray of oblique light, as well as the close-up, the working class faces, and the strong lighting, show how much this thirty-year-old painter knew the works of Caravaggio and Manfredi. The composition, which teems with figures, is solidly constructed: Christ is the central figure, the others being linked to him in a sweeping arabesque which gives the scene dramatic intensity, further increased by the deep chiaroscuro. To this lesson, drawn from the Roman school, Vignon adds stylistic characteristics of his own, such as his use of thick, gritty pigments, sometimes modelled with the tip of the brush, his glowing palette, in which he brings together blue, lilac and deep reds. The vigour of Vignon's execution, and his rich imagination, place him among the finest French Caravaggiesque painters of the first half of the 17th century, alongside Valentin de Boulogne and Georges de La Tour.

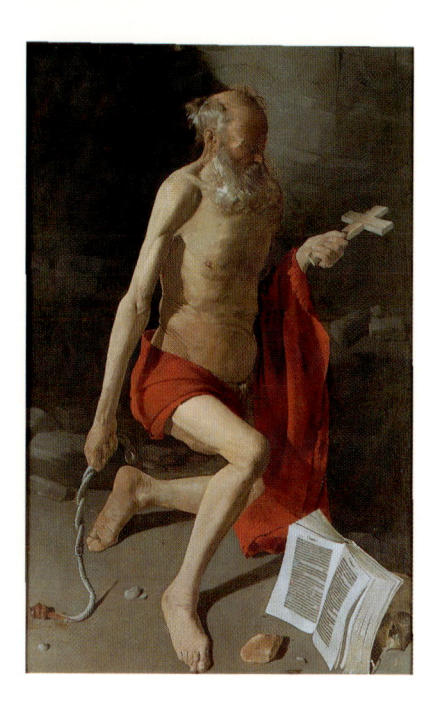

Saint Jerome

Georges de La Tour

c. 1639
Oil on canvas
157 x 100
Gift of the departmental authorities
of Isère in 1799

Vic sur Seille, 1593
Lunéville, 1652

Discovered in the Abbey of Saint Antoine en Viennois by L.-J. Jay, the first curator of the Museum of Grenoble, and catalogued in 1797 under the name of Ribera, this painting by Georges de La Tour, whose work only came back into favour during the 20th century, is one of the most remarkable masterpieces of the museum. It represents Saint Jerome, who, as a penitent, has removed his cardinal's vestments, and chosen to live naked in mortification. Neither the open Bible leaning again a skull, nor the crucifix in his hand hold his attention: he is lost in a state of adoration, and his whole body — the tall, straight torso, the long extended arm, the fist closed on a rope ending in a bloodstained knot, the leg bent at right angles — indicates a determination, described without harshness but with clinical precision, that is in no way tempered by his great age. In this barren space where a few stones are scattered, the figure of the old man is shown slightly lowered and, as André Chastel points out, appears to have been distorted to fit the format. The palette is cold, restricted to greys and ochres, with white, red, and the blue of the Bible's initial letters. All one's attention is taken up by the extraordinary arabesques of the body, long and slender in its trajectory, and of the sharp echoing shadows, as well as by the virtuosity of the pictorial technique, which leaves highlights standing out in the hair, and in the long beard descending into the hairs on the chest.

This great work, austere and intense, just where it appears to describe human decrepitude, in fact celebrates, in Jacques Thuillier's words, the "most secret mystery of spiritual certainties."

Claude Lorrain
(Claude Gellée)

Chamagne, 1600
Rome (Italy), 1682

Landscape at Tivoli with the Temple of the Sibyl

c. 1644
Oil on canvas
98 x 137
Acquired in 1719

This landscape is composed of real and imaginary elements observed in the Roman countryside. The right-hand side of the painting is an evocation of Tivoli (the building is the circular ruined temple of the Sibyl, and the five-arched bridge is the Ponte Molle or Milvio, where Constantine fought Maxentius). All this was carefully drawn *in situ*, and is shown here in such an idealized form that the landscape becomes a meditation on human destiny. The presence of the ruins imprints the effects of time on nature, with the observation of the morning light, and the human presence in the landscape, leading to a reflection on the succession of days and the relation between man and nature. The colours used by Claude Lorrain for his perspective rendering have been applied with such skill that he manages, by numerous gradations, to amplify the suggestion of space. People are brought into harmony with landscape elements through ideal correspondences of colour. In the words of Gilles Chomer: "The whole palette is dominated by the vast, implacable cadence of blue and yellow, present in the sky and embryonically inscribed in the two pure tones of the shepherdesses' clothes, then echoed in the red clothing of the cowherd on the bridge." This painting, whose theme is further expanded on by the existence, in Buckingham Palace, of a companion piece — a view at sunset — is of the type that founded the classical conception of landscape in Paris around 1650. Its value is enhanced by the fact that it was "painted for Mr Pasar", in remembrance of a walk at Tivoli: Mr Pasar, a scholar of the art of painting, was a patron of Poussin.

The Temptation of Saint Anthony

Simon Vouet

c. 1638-40
Oil on canvas
278 x 163
Presented by the State, 1799

Paris, 1550-1649

Painted for the chapel of the Saint Honoré Oratory in Paris, this large, theatrical canvas renews the traditional presentation of Saint Anthony's temptation: Vouet chose to represent the saint at the moment when Christ comes to his aid in the midst of his delirium, and stretches forth a soothing hand, while a winged creature takes flight upon catching sight of an angel. The composition thus opposes two registers, terrestrial and celestial, between two ascending, parallel obliques, two planes at different depths. The layered planes are animated by curves and countercurves, and, as there is only a moderate use of chiaroscuro, everything retains its essential shape, especially the objects on the ground. An art of the ellipse is brought into play, in keeping with the elegance and seriousness of the representation. The palette, dominated by yellow and tinted greys, is symbolic of the struggle between light and darkness.

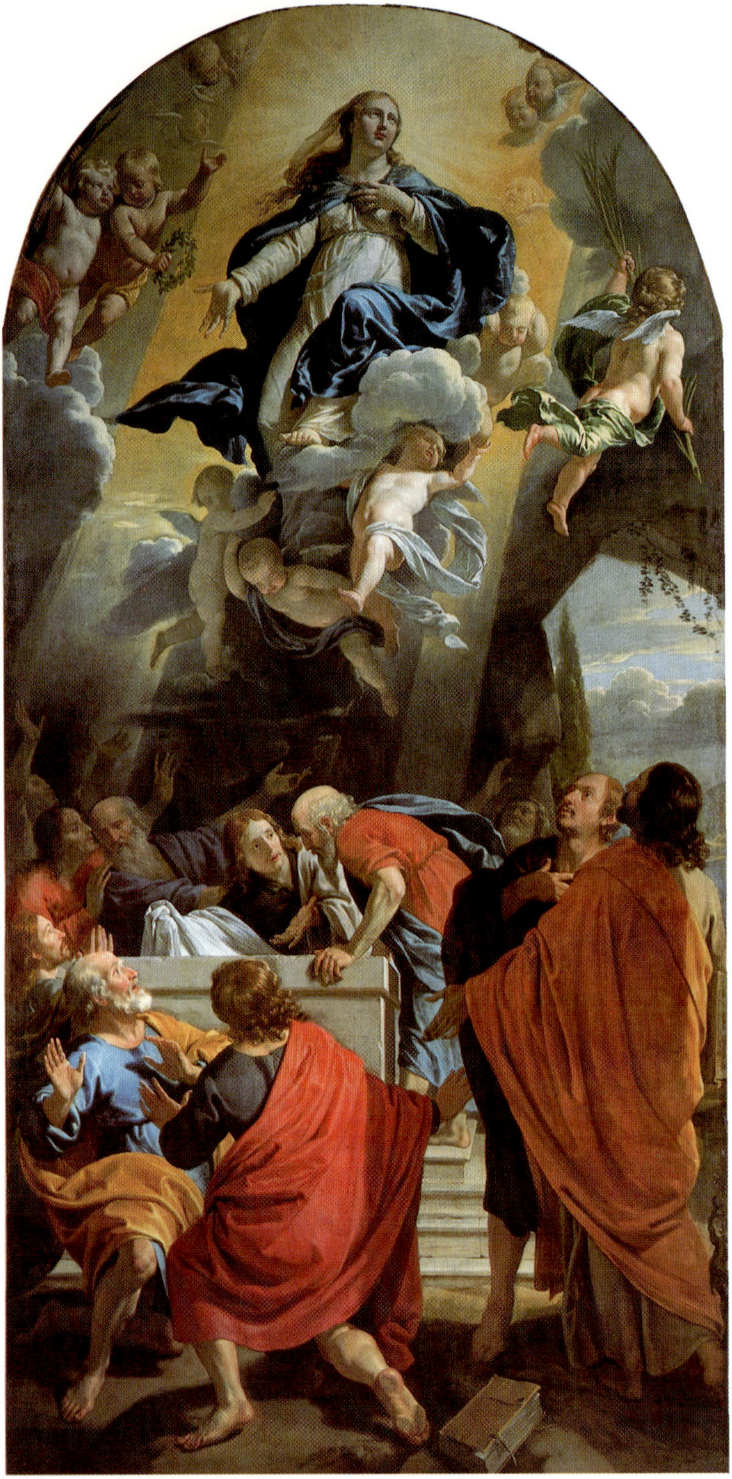

The Assumption

c. 1638-1640
Oil on canvas
351 x 179
Loaned by the State in 1799

Philippe de Champaigne

Brussels (Brabant), 1602
Paris, 1674

This work was painted for the Lady Chapel in the church of Saint Germain l'Auxerrois, in Paris. It is a faithful illustration of the Assumption of the Virgin as described by Jacobus de Voragine in the *Golden Legend*: the Virgin is carried heavenward by angels, one of them holding a palm of Paradise, in the presence of the eleven apostles. Two superposed planes are lit by the golden rays emanating from the Virgin. The terrestrial scene shows the apostles, whose faces express feelings ranging from astonishment to religious fervour. One single diagonal, linking the lower level, occupied by Saint John and Saint Peter, to the upper level, expresses the irresistible ascension of the Virgin. The glimpse of a landscape — with the dark vertical of a cypress echoing the tomb, and blending into a luminous sky — lightens this composition, which, despite its dynamism, remains stable. The influence of de Champaigne's Flemish culture can be seen in the light and its reflections, in the use of bright colours, and in the movement imparted to the scene through the divine rays, although the solid articulation of the volumes and groups, as well as the calm gestures, show that de Champaigne belonged, in fact, to the "Parisian Atticism" school.

Like *The Body of Christ on the Cross*, this portrait of Jean Duvergier de Hauranne, Abbot of Saint Cyran, is a magnificent example of the highly-skilled spiritual art of Philippe de Champaigne. The abbot is seen from the right, half-length, in three-quarters profile, behind a parapet, his strangely monolithic posture recalling a funeral bust. Weak directional lighting modulates the bare background — a dark grisaille — against which the face stands out. The portrait was done three or four years after the death of the abbot, from his plaster death mask and his friends' recollections, and yet we are made to feel the intense character of this great intellectual and religious figure, who was the true spiritual leader of Jansenism. The composition, deliberately reduced to its bare essentials, and the dry, precise technique, demonstrate the level of abstraction attained by the art of Philippe de Champaigne, who could induce the viewer to forget his technique, the better to serve his subject.

Portrait of the Abbot of Saint Cyran

1646-1647 (?)
Oil on canvas
73 x 58
Acquired in 1823

The Body of Christ on the Cross

1655
Oil on canvas
222.8 x 192
Gift of the departmental authorities of Isère in 1799

Philippe de Champaigne, official painter of Louis XIII and Louis XIV, appreciated by the aristocracy as well as by the Church, produced a large number of works in a variety of genres, for a variety of uses. It appears that the works where his genius is shown at its best are those in which he expresses his sense of spirituality and his austere sensibility: *The Body of Christ on the Cross* is one such work. Commissioned by the Carthusian order, with whom he always retained strong links, the work was painted for the Grande Chartreuse, near Grenoble. The composition is reduced as far as possible: the canvas is divided up into four equal parts, frontal shapes follow the frame, the technique is abstract; this painting is a perfect example of Classicism. The drama of Christ's death is expressed in the slight setting off of the cross, picked up by the unidirectional lighting, and in the position of the crosspiece, so high up that it almost touches the upper edge of the painting. Such an austere colour scale, the luminism of the solar eclipse, the analytical drawing, and the abstract void of the space constitute an invitation to the contemplative life and inner asceticism.

Laurent de La Hyre

Paris, 1606-1656

Christ Appearing to the Pilgrims at Emmaus

1656
Oil on canvas
162 x 175
Gift of the departmental authorities of Isère in 1799

This painting and its companion piece, *Christ Appearing to Mary Magdalene*, were La Hyre's last commission. They were painted for two chapels of the Grande Chartreuse, near Grenoble, one year after Philippe de Champaigne's *The Body of Christ on the Cross*. Constructed along rigorous, mathematical lines, this representation of the disciples at Emmaus is dominated by the orthogonality of the forms and their relation to the frame. Thus, the group formed by Christ and the disciples is inscribed in a rectangle solidly structured by flat surfaces of colour and parallel to the plane of the canvas, which is limited on the left by the two vertical columns of the temple, and on the right by the door of a house. The only oblique lines, those of the banisters and the foliage, are stopped at both extremities in such a way that the eye is trapped within the composition. This tension, created by purposeful geometry, and addressing itself to the viewer's intelligence, is compensated for by the evocation of a broad landscape surrounding the religious scene: a natural landscape with luxurious vegetation enclosing an architectural landscape humanized by a few busy figures painted in pale, delicate, transparent colours. This calm, serene masterpiece, which was only finished in the year of the painter's death, places La Hyre — who was rediscovered when his work was exhibited in Grenoble, in 1988 — on a par with the most accomplished masters of Classicism.

The Angel Raphael Taking Leave of Tobiah and his Family

Eustache Le Sueur

Paris, 1616-1655

c. 1647
Oil on canvas
173 x 215
Acquired between 1824 and 1830

This work is one of a series of panels illustrating the life of Tobiah, commissioned for the Hôtel de Fieubet in Paris and painted around 1647. It was most probably the central panel of one of the ceilings, and was placed close to another, smaller panel. *The Return of Tobiah*, which is now in the Louvre. It should not be forgotten, when examining the format, composition, and technique, that the canvas was not meant to be seen on its own. Le Sueur shows here his perfect mastery of the art of perspective, linear as well as atmospheric, which led to a heated debate at the time. The scene, viewed from below, is extremely solid and architectural, comprising the base and the shafts of the columns of a Doric temple, and the steps leading up to it.

In the pure, austere framework that represents the habitation of Tobiah and his family, their appearance — prostrate in an attitude of total humility and fervour — which is echoed by the goat and bouquetin nearby, is extraordinarily poetic, and this is confirmed by the pastel tones and glaze of the clear colours, acidulous even in certain parts of the sky, that gives the scene a unique, subtle freshness. There are signs of a real genius for decorative art: it is not difficult to imagine the gaiety that such panels brought to the rooms they adorned, where they must have been seen as a glorification of light.

School of Charles Le Brun

Mary Magdalene in the Desert

c. 1656-1657
Oil on canvas
358 x 255
Loaned by the State in 1799

This work, which was painted for the Carmelite church in the Rue Saint Jacques in Paris, is dedicated to the worship of Mary Magdalene, common in the 17th century. The saint is represented as a penitent, with the instruments of her mortification, in the cave of Sainte Baume, near the abbey of Saint Maximin. The thistle, with its wide, fleshy leaves, has a multiple symbolic value: its spines evoke the crown of thorns and Christ's Passion, and it is a plant that represents immortality (due to the fact that it does not wilt), as well as withdrawal from the world (due to the way in which it takes over fallow land). The thistle is also a symbol of the Virgin because certain of its varieties secrete a milky juice). The work was probably based on a drawing or a sketch by Charles Le Brun, and painted by a student of his, with the master applying the final brushstrokes. The arch at the top of the canvas can be explained by the original position of the painting in the vault of the chapel. The detail is fascinating: the delicious expression of sadness on the face of the saint, the meticulous rendering of her hair, the superb loading of colour used for the face, the carefully-observed touches of realism. But the most striking effect of the composition is the importance given to the landscape, a genre rarely attempted by Le Brun himself; here it is highly poetical, as well as innovative, notably in the topography of the cave surrounded by mountains, the morning light used to harden contrasts, the incorporation of a large reclining figure into a vertical format, the prominence of the thistle, and the hint of chalkiness that runs across the entire palette.

The Martyrdom of Saint Ovid

Jean-Baptiste Jouvenet

1690
Oil on canvas
267 x 176
Presented by the State, 1799

Rouen, 1644
Paris, 1717

Jean-Baptiste Jouvenet is the most famous member of a family of painters and sculptors from Rouen. He specialized almost exclusively in religious paintings, and this one was commissioned for a chapel in the convent of the Capuchins, in Paris. The scene, viewed from just below, is a rigorous diagonal arrangement of figures radiating outward from Saint Ovid, who is standing in the centre; the tumultuous terrestrial world, shown against an architectural background, is opposed to the lightness of the celestial world. The triangular construction of the foreground is clearly brought out, with prominent figures painted in large surfaces of primary colours producing strong formal contrasts (e.g. the broken line formed by the man sitting on the right, and the long curve of the mother on the left); this solemn, monumental work abounds in realistic descriptions, such as the carefully observed weapons and the perfect orange-pink harmony of the draperies, as well as the joined hands of the man sitting on the right. The upper part, where an angel appears in a swarm of cherubim, is an intense chromatic variation of radiating yellow, echoed by the intense blue of the sky showing through the clouds. In this large decorative scene, the bold construction is tempered by the elegance and lyricism of the colours.

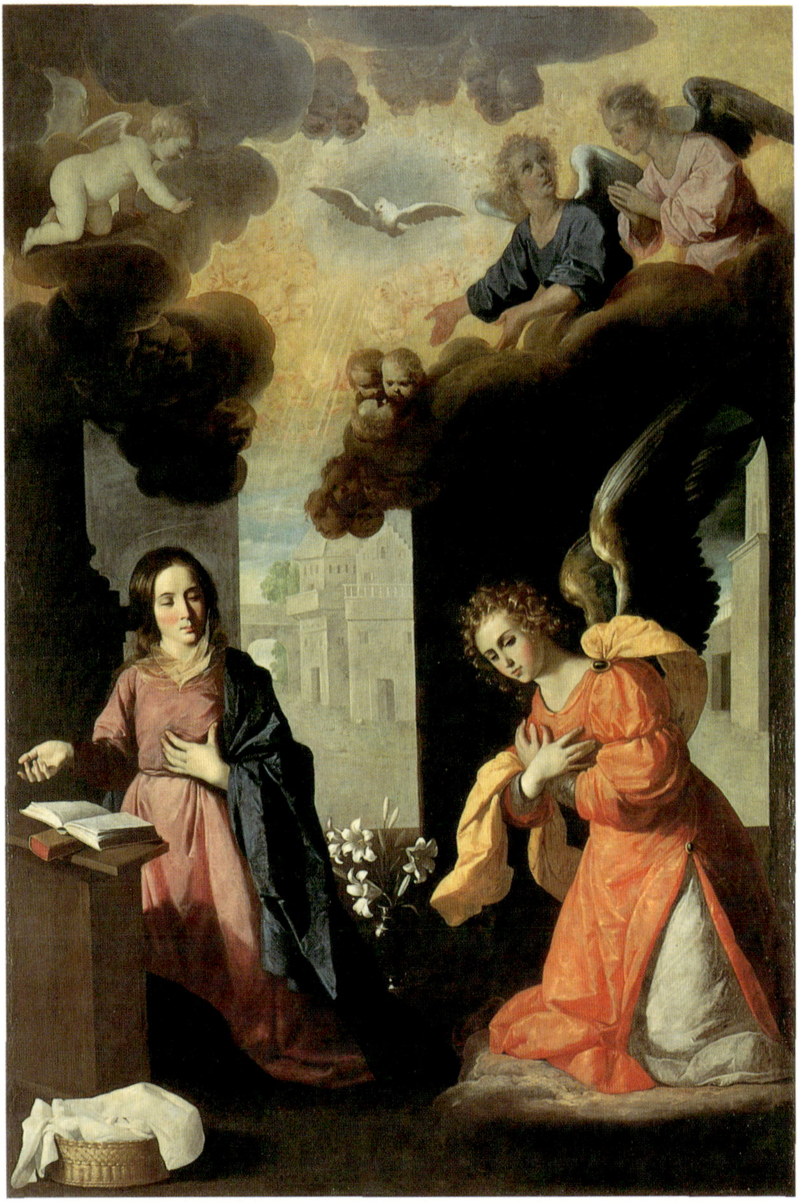

The Annunciation

Oil on canvas
267 x 185
Gift of General de Beylié, 1904

Francisco de Zurbarán

Fuente de Cantos (Spain), 1598
Madrid (Spain), 1664

Zurbarán ranks alongside Velasquez and Murillo as one of the greatest painter of the Spanish "Golden Century". The four Zurbaran paintings in the Museum of Grenoble were executed between 1638 and 1639, and come from the retable in the Carthusian monastery of Jerez de la Frontera. The central panel, illustrating *The Battle of Jerez* (an episode from medieval Spanish history) is now in the New York Metropolitan Museum. The Grenoble paintings were placed on two levels, on either side of the central panel, *The Annunciation* on the left and *The Adoration of the Shepherds* on the right; above left was *The Adoration of the Magi*, and above right, *The Circumcision*. Below, level with the altar, stood the figures of Saint John the Baptist and Saint Lawrence (now in the Museum of Cadiz). The retable was dismantled in 1837 and the panels now in Grenoble, acquired by General de Beylié in 1904, were immediately donated to the Museum. Their most striking quality is their monumental composition, the figures in each case being placed in a shallow space in the foreground. The forms are given solidity through the precise outlines and modelling of the volumes. The overall effect relies heavily on the use of chiaroscuro, and the light brings out the forms in expressive relief. Paradoxically, the overall dark cast does not exclude the use of colour in specific areas; patches of pink, yellow, orange and, more rarely, blue, emerge from the dark background, and give the composition a vibrant effect, while brilliant whites, for example that of the lilies in *The Annunciation*, and the sheet on which the Infant is laid in *The Adoration of the Shepherds*, draw the viewer's attention to specific areas. The larger-than-life quality of the figures is combined with a minute rendering of details, as is shown in the handling of the accessories — clothes and various other objects — that fill the paintings. Some of the still lifes, such as in *The Adoration of the Magi*, are fascinating on account of the meticulous technique displayed by the painter. Zurbarán's sense of action (in *The Annunciation*), theatrical staging (*The Adoration of the Magi*), naturalism (*The Adoration of the Shepherds*), and dramatic expressiveness (*The Circumcision*) are a clear indication of his debt to Mannerism, and to the art of Caravaggio; these qualities enabled him to build a universe where forms and colours dominate.

The Adoration of the Shepherds

Oil on canvas
267 x 185
Gift of General de Beylié, 1904

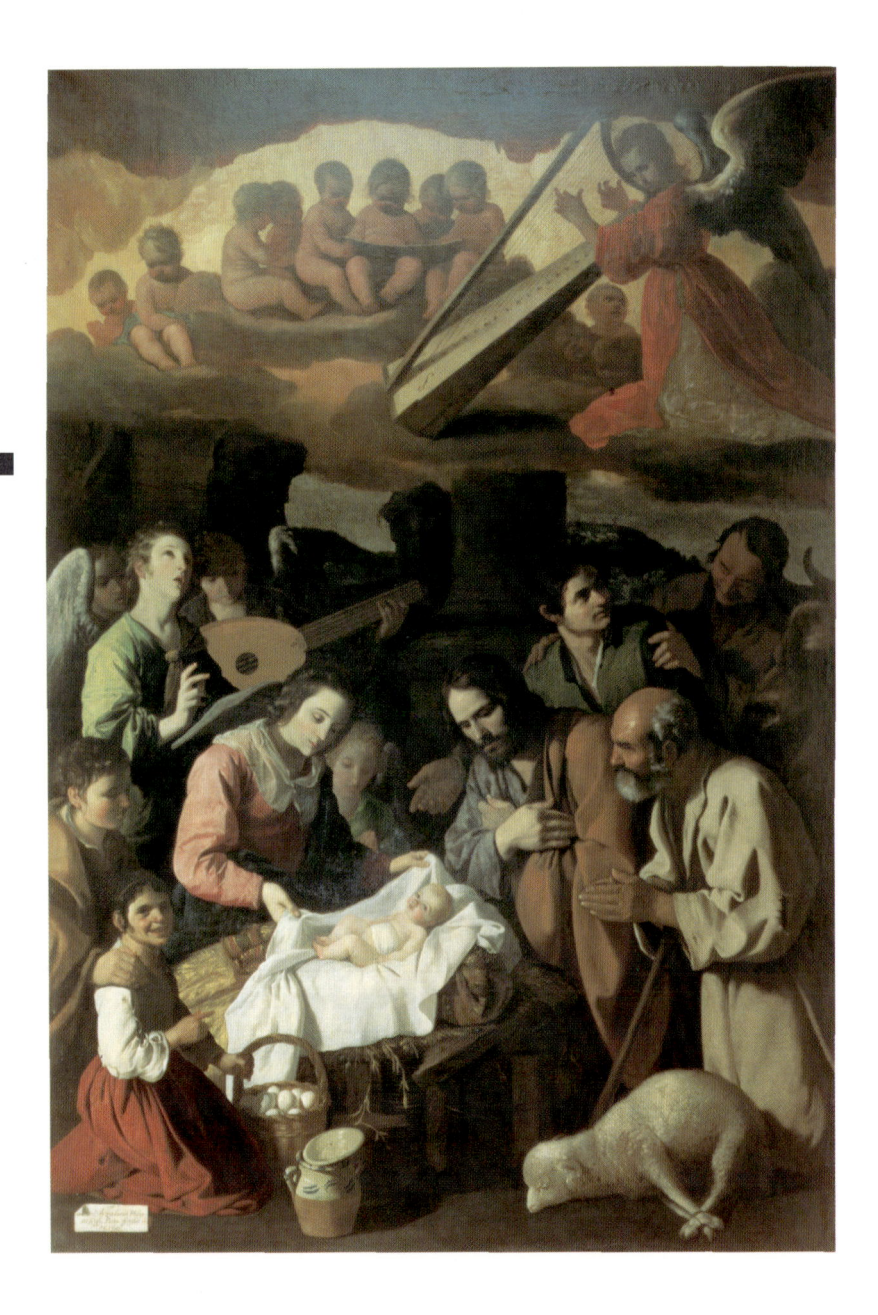

18TH CENTURY WORKS

Rooms 11 to 14

Ancient Art

Nicolas de Largillière

Paris, 1656-1746

Portrait of Jean Pupil de Craponne

1708
Oil on canvas
83 x 69
Acquired in 1833

This is one of the most famous paintings by de Largillière, a celebrated portraitist of the 18th century, whose main rival was Rigaud. The demand for portraits had considerably increased after the rise of the bourgeoisie, and the genre, until then considered as being of minor significance, was recognized by the Académie Royale. Little is known of the gentleman in ceremonial dress (who also commissioned a portrait of his wife). The composition is of amazing simplicity — the half-length figure takes up most the canvas, facing the viewer, his body at a slight angle. The extraordinary colour modulation and brilliant technique stand out: in the brown-red cloak, whose sharp folds are emphasized by streaks of white and gold (reminiscent of Rembrandt); and in the pictorial freedom of the night-blue sky and russet trees in the background. The graphic and colour virtuosity in draughtsmanship and colour conveys the tranquil insolence and splendour of the old gentleman.

The Martyrdom of Saint Andrew

1749
Oil on canvas
360 x 235
Presented by the State, 1799

Jean Restout

Rouen, 1692
Paris, 1768

Ancient Art

Jean Restout, born in Rouen like his uncle and teacher Jean-Baptiste Jouvenet, had a brilliant career in Paris. He was rediscovered in 1970 at an exhibition of his work in Rouen. *The Martyrdom of Saint Andrew*, his most celebrated masterpiece, was commissioned by the Collegiate Church of Saint Andrew in Grenoble. The composition is based on intersecting diagonals, with the figures arranged around Saint Andrew, who occupies the centre of the canvas. A certain mannerism can be detected in the elongated figures and the complicated, elegant postures. As with Jean-Baptiste Jouvenet, the draughtsmanship and fascination with objects can be seen in the magnificent treatment of draperies and the arrangement of objects in the foreground. The surface of the painting is done in a rich camaïeu of ochre and grey tones, with light, supple pigments characteristic of Restout's technique. The lyricism and majesty of the work, unmistakably Baroque, derive mainly from the representation and rendering of light in a stormy sky. This huge decorative canvas is made even more monumental by its sculpted frame, the work of a skilled craftsman.

François Desportes

Champigneulles, 1661
Paris, 1743

Animals, Flowers and Fruit

1717
Oil on canvas
124 x 231
Presented by the State, 1799

This painting, which was commissioned by the Regent, together with a companion piece, *Ducks, Pheasant and Fruit beside a Fountain* (now in the Museum of Lyon), once hung in the dining room of the château de la Muette, at the edge of the Bois de Boulogne. Desportes, then at the height of his art, organized the various parts of the painting with a solid sense of composition and a magnificent use of diagonals. In this seemingly haphazard congeries of animals, flowers and fruit, the painter's feeling for narrative enables him to make symbols out of elements and meanings. The painstaking technique, reminiscent of Flemish art and of that of Desportes' master, Rigaud, is shown in the precise rendering of textures and in the fine description of objects. All these qualities explain Desportes' success in creating such a sumptuous image, in the taste of decorative opulence characteristic of the French Regency period.

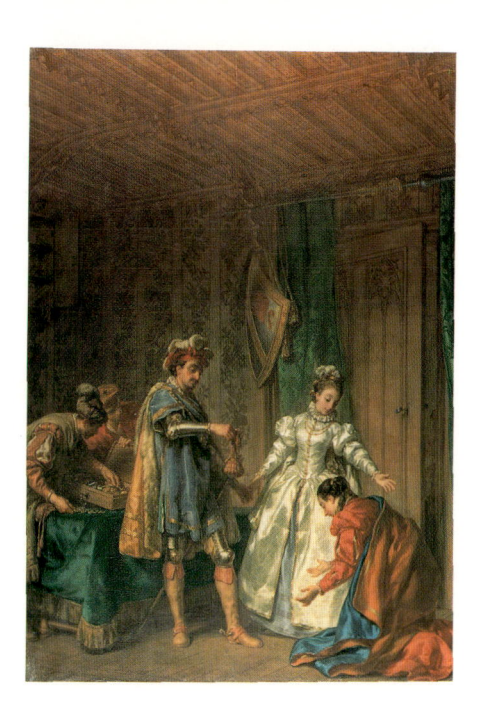

The Continence of Bayard

1775
Oil on canvas
323 x 227
Presented by the State, 1876

Louis-Jean-Jacques Durameau

Paris, 1733
Versailles, 1796

This painting was commissioned by Louis XVI's Superintendent of Buildings, with the intention of illustrating the "noble and virtuous actions that have marked our history." It shows an episode in the life of Bayard, the knight "without fear or reproach", while he was in Grenoble, where he was born in 1475; Bayard finds in his moral nobility the courage to resist desire, and to save the honour of a young woman, whom he provides with a rich dowry just as she is on the point of sacrificing her virtue for the money she needs to fly to the aid of her mother. This magnificent moral subject is a pretext for a new kind of re-creation of history: the commitment to archaeological truth is shown in the details of the Gothic room, in the exact heraldic representation of the coat of arms on Bayard's shield, and in the historically authentic clothes. The use of anecdotes drawn from daily life was a new development for historical painting, in this case the detail of the cupboard — where the purse was kept — whose door has been left ajar, with the key still in the lock. In this respect Durameau is ahead of his time: fifty years later the "troubadour" style was to illustrate recent history (mainly that of the Middle Ages and Renaissance) with small, highly-glazed genre paintings; but Durameau's technique, and his use of such a large format — normally reserved for great historical subjects — belong squarely to the 18th century. The Grenoble painting is an invaluable testimony to a transition between two periods, that of Boucher and that of David.

Nicolas-Guy Brenet

Paris, 1728-1792

The Death of Saint Joseph

1773
Oil on canvas
250 x 152
Gift of the departmental authorities
of Isère in 1799

Brenet produced a number of paintings in the Lyon region, and it was from a convent in La Tour du Pin that this canvas was taken during the Revolution. Its subject, the death of Saint Joseph, has rarely been painted. Brenet stuck faithfully to the account given in an apocryphal gospel of the 4th century: the Virgin is sitting at the foot of the bed, Christ at the head, and cherubs have dressed Saint Joseph in a white robe. This work was painted during Brenet's mature years, and the clear separation of the masses, the frozen gestures, as well as the powerful vertical lines, compose a peaceful image, full of classical feeling. Realistic details, such as the sandals, and the peg-joined wood of the platform, and also the rustically simple construction of the platform itself share in the new spirit which pervaded French painting during the years 1750-1760, and which led to the art of David.

The Rape of Proserpine

Joseph-Marie Vien

1767
Oil on canvas
320 x 320
Presented by the State, 1873

Montpellier, 1716
Paris, 1809

This large, square painting is a cartoon for a tapestry that was commissioned to illustrate the amorous escapades of the gods. The artist chose to evoke, not the actual carrying off of Proserpine by Pluto, but "one brief instant," as described by Ovid, "enough for Pluto to see, fall in love with and abduct her"; this took place as the goddess was placing flowers at the foot of her mother's statue. The tapestry was woven in a number of different versions at the Gobelins, first during the reign of Louis XIV, and then, during the Revolution. Vien was the most innovative of the four artists commissioned to do the complete hanging. In this composition, the forms stand out, and emphasis is given to the verticals, which are strongly articulated by diagonal and oblique lines. To the novelty of such a simple arrangement has been added a feeling for archæological references, as is clearly shown in the antique style of the draperies, the shape of the vase, and the plinth of the statue, which bears a Greek inscription. The light palette is perfectly suited to a tapestry transcription. This painting marks the inception of the change in taste brought about by the rediscovery of Greek art, which influenced French painting and ushered in a new style.

Jean-Antoine Houdon

Barnave

Versailles, 1741
Paris, 1828

Terra-cotta
75 x 50 x 27, including base
Gift of the Comte de Bouchange, 1851

Houdon is one of the greatest portraitists in the history of sculpture. His bust of Barnave is one of a series depicting famous men of the Revolutionary age. Antoine Barnave was a barrister at the Parliament of Grenoble, the town where he was born in 1761. He was a member of the États du Dauphiné, which assembled in Vizille in 1788, then a representative of the Tiers État at the États Généraux in 1789; he was guillotined during the Terror, in 1793. Houdon's portrait, done in the classical fashion, with drapery, shows Barnave in a three-quarters movement of the head, his gaze directed upwards, as if addressing the viewer, with an expression that captures the model's vitality. This perfectly accomplished study in psychological expression is combined with a realistic description of the materials depicted: the soft folds of the toga, the lively lines of the curls, the sensitive treatment of the skin.

This is a work in which the overall, strongly baroque dynamic of the composition and the treatment of textures, are tempered by a Neoclassical influence.

Monks at Prayer, Tempted by the Devil

Oil on canvas
97 x 72
Acquired in 1844

Sebastiano Ricci
(attrib.)

Belluno (Italy), 1653
Venice (Italy), 1734

The inspiration for this painting is drawn from a subject frequently illustrated by the Genovese painter Alessandro Magnasco (1667-1749), who was apparently the inventor of this genre which evokes the solitary life of anchorite monks, although the realism of the rocky background, and the particular features of the painter's touch are typical of Ricci's work. The baroque composition organizes the bodies along two major diagonals, the sky being partly hidden by rocky masses shaped like a leaning cross, from which springs a naked woman. The elongated figures are shown in forceful postures, to which the vibrant gradations from light to dark appear to lend movement. The sharp brushstrokes sculpt the forms with thick blobs of paint that catch the light. This work, which is characteristic of Ricci's artistic education, was painted in the 18th century, in the middle of the Baroque period. It demonstrates that the artist has assimilated the Mannerist experiments, which he applies to an elegant form of expressionism.

Giovanni Paolo Pannini

Saint Peter Preaching to the Romans

Piacenza (Italy), 1691
Rome (Italy), 1765

1742
Oil on canvas
61 x 74
Acquired between 1824 and 1830

This painting is a clear example of the 18th century taste for landscapes featuring historical ruins. Recognizable here are the remaining columns of the temple of Castor and Pollux in the Roman Forum, the pyramid of Caius Sextus, an antique bas-relief showing a nymph pursued by a satyr, and one of the Egyptian lions of the Aqua Felice fountain (now in the Vatican Museum). All these elements, brought together in an arbitrary way and lit by flashes of light, provide a theatrical background to the narrative, whose protagonists are painted in strange groups and attitudes.

The Dogana and Santa Maria della Salute as Seen from the Jetty

Canaletto
(Giovanni Antonio Canal)

Venice (Italy), 1697-1768

c. 1726-1728
Oil on canvas
191 x 203
Acquired in 1840

This landscape illustrates the balance between human constructions and nature that has been achieved at one of the most representative places in Venice, the entrance to the Canal Grande. Looking out, as it were, from the stone balustrade and wooden pier in the foreground, one sees, on the right, the Fontighetto della Farina (since demolished) and, on the other side of the canal, the tall tower of the Dogana, as well as the basilica of Santa Maria della Salute with its characteristic volutes. In the background, part of the Giudecca is visible; to the left, the church of San Giovanni Battista (now also demolished); and, at the centre, the church of Il Redentore by Andrea Palladio.

Through the use of this viewpoint, Canaletto has opened up a broad panoramic horizon, where buildings and people are reduced in scale, with a wide expanse of canal and lagoon, and a broad expanse of sky that takes up over half of the painting. The light comes from the left, and is suggestive of the early morning. Pale greys dominate the palette, with warmer colours lighting up a few buildings and occurring also in the bright yellow, red and blue tones of the figures' clothes. A clever use of the long oblique line of the embankment draws us into the painting from the bottom left-hand corner, so that we are made to contemplate, like the small figure in blue leaning against the balustrade, this moment of beauty enclosed in the most propitious format for expressing harmony: the square.

Francesco Guardi

Venice (Italy), 1712-1792

The Newly-Elected Doge of Venice Being Carried by Gondoliers through the Piazza San Marco

Oil on canvas
67 x 100
Presented by the State, 1811

This painting is one of a series of twelve works illustrating the ceremonies that marked the election of Doge Alvise IV Mocenigo in 1763. The series, which began immediately after the publication, in 1766, of the set of prints by Brustolon which were used by Guardi, was finished a few years later, and is considered to be the artist's greatest masterpiece. Here, the Doge is throwing coins to the crowd while being carried on men's backs across the Piazza San Marco; gondoliers armed with long staffs clear a path for him. The perspective view of the piazza, culminating in the basilica and filled with people, shows Guardi's mastery of composition, while his virtuosity at narrative description enables him to combine his virtuosity in depicting sweeping views with a feeling for the smallest details, through the clever use of light and colour

*Snowy Landscape
with Rocks and Travellers*

Francesco Foschi

Ancona (Italy), (?)
Rome (Italy), *c.* 1805

1750
Oil on canvas
48 x 74
Acquired in 1799

Only about ten paintings can be attributed with certainty to Foschi; this landscape, painted in 1750, gave us the name of the painter's birthplace, which was written on the back. The theme — a snowy landscape — appears to have been one of the painter's favourites. It was illustrated for the first time in Italy by Marco Ricci, and it is likely that Foschi drew his inspiration from Ricci's painting. The work is dominated by minute, realistic description of people and the landscape, and heralds the objective æstheticism of Neoclassicism.

19TH CENTURY WORKS

Rooms 15 to 24

Study of a Woman's Head

Jacques-Louis David
(attrib.)

c. 1780
Oil on canvas
48 x 40
Bequest of Mme Fantin-Latour, 1926

Paris, 1748
Brussels (Belgium), 1825

This work belonged to Henri Fantin-Latour; it is not known whether he acquired it himself or whether he inherited it from his father; both father and son had studied under a follower of David, and the painting shown here obviously influenced Fantin-Latour's own work; as such, it is a prized possession of the museum; though it was left in the form of a study, its brilliant execution is plastically thought-provoking: subtly not-quite-primary colours sketch out the complexion and the hair, going from bluish grey to russet brown, with pinks, reds and mauves, while golden greys and beiges are used for the background and the clothes. A vibrant touch is used with the thicker paint of the dress, while the precise rendering enhances the geometry of parts of the face. The frozen movement of the bust, and the fiery expression of the face, with its dilated pupils, are full of emotion; this unforgettable work has now been dated with some certainty to David's early years, around 1780.

Girodet

(Anne-Louis Girodet de Roucy-Trioson)

Montargis, 1767
Paris, 1824

*Portrait of
Benjamin Rolland*

1816
Oil on canvas
64 x 53
Acquired in 1847

The name of Benjamin Rolland is well known in Grenoble due to his having been the second curator of the museum, a position to which he was appointed in 1817, in succession to Louis-Joseph Jay; he was at the same time the director of the school of drawing. A creole from Martinique, he was described by the journalist Louis-Charles Delescluze as "quick-tempered but not malevolent", and also "honest, courageous and witty"; he was a student of David around 1796, and was called "Le Furieux" by the other students. Two of his paintings are in the museum; one of them was thought by Stendhal to be "atrocious". This portrait by Girodet shows him at the age of about forty. The treatment of the strong-featured massive head and the white cravat is complete, while the background is no more than the white preparation of the support, on which the clothes and hair have merely been sketched out. The portrait was painted hastily, in a few sittings, and shows Girodet's desire to express the inner truth of his model, in an unaffected way. The "outlining" frames with great integrity the moral portrait of the model.

Portrait of Isabelle Gaudry, née Hittorf

Jean-Auguste-Dominique Ingres

1864
Oil on canvas
33 x 33
Loaned by the State in 1976

Montauban, 1780
Paris, 1867

This portrait represents Isabelle Hittorf, daughter of the architect Jacques-Ignace Hittorf (1792-1867) and wife of Albert Gaudry, a famous paleontologist. The model is seen frontally, with her eyes slightly lowered and her hair parted in the middle to form two smooth bandeaux. The rigorous frontal view emphasizes a symmetry that subjugates the form to the frame, which it fills entirely. The tip of the nose is thus the exact centre of the circular painting, and the long curves of the arched eyebrows, the hair and the outline of the face are important parts of the composition, cancelling the modelling of the face. The geometry and stylization of Mme Gaudry's face exert the strong fascination of a mask, and give her the implacable appearance of a goddess. This portrait was later used by Ingres when he painted a series of six medallions representing the principal gods for the decoration of Hittorf's apartment. His *Minerva*, now housed at the Wallraf-Richartz Museum in Cologne, was inspired by the features of Isabelle Hittorf.

Clémence-Sophie de Sermézy

The Return of the Prodigal Son

Lyon 1767
Charentay, 1850

Terra-cotta
25 x 26.5 x 11.2
Gift of the Société des Amis
du Musée de Grenoble, 1991

Clémence-Sophie de Sermézy was particularly fond of small formats, executed mostly in terra-cotta, whose originality lay in the importance given to groups and their realistic treatment. This terra-cotta is highly representative of her art, which is close to that of the so-called "troubadour" style of painting practised by the Lyonnais artists Revoil and Richard. The theme is drawn from the Bible, but the scale of the figures, their posture, and the careful rendering of details, force the viewer to minute observation and to an imaginary transposition of the Biblical subject into everyday life. The staging of religious feeling is subtly brought out through plastic means alone.

Rogero Delivering Angelica

Eugène Delacroix

Oil on canvas
46 x 55
Acquired in 1858

Saint Maurice, 1798
Paris, 1863

Delacroix found the inspiration for this small canvas, which was painted around 1855-1858, in *Orlando Furioso*, by Ariosto, the celebrated Renaissance poet. The subject, which had already been made famous by other painters, especially Ingres, thirty years before Delacroix, is that of Rogero delivering Angelica, who is chained to a storm-beaten rock and menaced by a dragon. The masterly treatment of the paint surface is characteristic of the leader of the Romantic school: the thick pigment shows the marks left by the brush, which the painter handles with great energy, as if he wanted to express the disturbing aspect of the scene through the texture of the pigments as well as by his choice of colours. The shapes, rather than being drawn, have been modelled in colours, at least if drawing is considered as a question of abstract distinct lines marking out shapes. The harmonies of green, combined here and there with cerulean blue and red, are characteristic of Delacroix's palette.

Ary Scheffer

Dordrecht (Netherlands), 1795
Argenteuil, 1858

Self-portrait

1830
Oil on canvas
118 x 90
Gift of General de Beylié, 1901

This painting is thought to be a self-portrait. The subject is shown wearing a roomy red dressing gown, his face highlighted by the white collar of his shirt, and indeed by the entire composition. The palette, the stretcher and the pencil holder in the hand indicate the sitter's profession. The face is shown frontally, and, from behind a small pairs of glasses, the almost questioning eyes look straight out at the viewer, with a serious, intense expression, making this portrait a symbol of the Romantic artist. The fully-developed technique, with rapidly-executed reds, care taken with the face, shows the range of the painter's art, which, together with the insight afforded by the portrait, gives the key to the success enjoyed by Scheffer, who received numerous commissions from Louis Philippe; today he is unjustly forgotten.

Hercules and Lycas

1820
Oil on canvas
325 x 272
Presented by the State, 1822

Jean-Baptiste Mauzaisse

Corbeil, 1784
Paris, 1844

The painting illustrates an episode in the life of Hercules, as recounted in Ovid's *Metamorphoses*: Hercules has been poisoned by the blood of the centaur Nessus, which was used to impregnate the tunic of Deianeira, his jealous wife, brought to him by Lycas. Maddened by pain and anger, he throws Lycas into the sea. However, Mauzaisse was not so much inspired by Ovid's text as by Canova's sculpture on the same theme, which exalted the gesture of the hero. Marked by Neoclassicism, Mauzaisse pays particular attention to the drawing of the arabesques formed by the bodies, and to the composition of the scene, reduced to its essential features: the contrast between forms, a few details — such as the overturned altar on which Hercules was ready to place the hide of the lion of Nemea, as a sacrifice to Jupiter — and the light of the full moon, which simplifies the landscape and freezes the uncontrasted colours.

Alexandre Laemlein

Hoenfeld (Bavaria), 1813
Pontlevoy, 1871

Jacob's Ladder

1847
Oil on canvas
455 x 325
Loaned by the State in 1873

Born in Germany, Alexandre Laemlein studied in Paris at the École des Beaux-Arts — in the studios of Regnault and Picot. He rapidly acquired a reputation for his mural paintings, and became a specialist in religious subjects. *Jacob's Ladder* was shown at the Salon of 1847, where the public was astonished by the iconography, the composition, the palette, the format and the technique. In the Biblical account, Jacob, the ancestor of the twelve tribes of Israel, has a dream, in which he sees angels ascending and descending a ladder, while God blesses Jacob's descendants. Laemlein took what was almost an opposing view of this episode: God is shown descending the ladder and advancing towards Jacob, who may be asleep, but is in the throes of a violent agitation. The pyramidal composition is meant to emphasize the celestial figures, which are painted in grisaille and strongly modelled. The painting's fantastical aspect is due to the vertical axis of symmetry, the play of light, and the frontal treatment of the main characters, Jacob excepted. This vision, strongly reminiscent of mythical Nordic scenes, can be compared to Ingres' *Ossian's Dream*; the impression of power is increased by the size of the work, which is the largest in the museum's possessions.

Scottish Lake after a Storm

1875-1878
Oil on canvas
90 x 130
Gift of Dr. Fuzier, 1880

Gustave Doré

Strasbourg, 1832
Paris, 1883

Ancient Art

Although better known for his work as an illustrator, in which he developed a previously-unknown form of social realism, Gustave Doré thought of himself primarily as a painter, devoting himself to landscapes, such as the painting seen here, and to Biblical scenes. It was on his return from his first trip to Scotland, in 1873, that he painted *Scottish Lake after a Storm*, the most Romantic of all his landscapes. The real setting, such as he had observed it, is transformed into an imaginary world by his use of a strange lighting, the play of the mist and clouds shrouding the mountain tops, the droplet-like brushstrokes, and the earthy colours and acid tones of the palette. In this landscape, "special effects" endow the painting with animal power, and create a wholly original fantastical vision.

James Pradier
(Jean-Jacques Pradier)

Geneva (Switzerland), 1790
Bougival, 1852

Phryne

1845
Parian marble, traces of colour and gold
183 x 40 x 47
Jules Monnet-Daiguenoire bequest, 1903

After studying with Neoclassical artists, Pradier, whose favourite theme was feminine beauty, created a scandal in 1834 with the Romanticism of his *Satyr and Bacchante*. In *Phryne*, Neoclassicism and Romanticism are brought together. Phryne was a Greek Courtesan who was accused of impiety by the Areopagus but was acquitted when her defender displayed her body; from this episode Pradier retains only the interiorized grace of the courtesan, who is shown alone, without her protector. The position of her arms and hips, the inclination of her head, and the fold of her dress — which draw the light and shadows towards her body — are indications of meditation and restraint, not wanton insolence. The silent presence of this work, which was roughed out in twenty-six hours, was praised by Baudelaire for its exquisite charm.

Frédéric-Auguste Bartholdi

Colmar, 1834
Paris, 1904

Champollion

1867
Plaster
200 x 70 x 70
Gift of Mme Bartholdi, 1904

After Bartholdi's trip to Egypt and the coast of the Indian Ocean, it was natural that the artist should be commissioned to execute a sculpture in honour of Jean-François Champollion, the Egyptologist. The final work, sculpted in marble, was originally destined for the town of Figeac, where Champollion was born in 1790, but was presented by the State to the Collège de France in 1876. Champollion had been a pupil at the Lycée de Grenoble, and went back to the town to take up a chair of history. This is why Bartholdi's widow gave the town the plaster sculpture seen here, which was used as a model for the final marble version at the Collège de France. Exhibited at the Universal Exhibition of 1867, it received an enthusiastic description in the *Journal illustré*:

"It would be impossible to render with more striking truth the state of deep meditation of the scientist as he faces the mystery so many before him had tried in vain to interpret, and which his genius was to unravel. Gazing at this Sphinx's head, (...) Champollion is tracing out in his mind a train of thought in which truth has started to appear; and his foot, placed on a dumb witness of the past whose silence he has decided to transform into speech, is already a sign of his triumph." This work is one of the most important in the museum's sculpture collection; it shows how the author of *Liberty Enlightening the World*, in New York, was renewing the art of sculpture through his feeling for the monumental, and his ability to turn an effigy into a symbol.

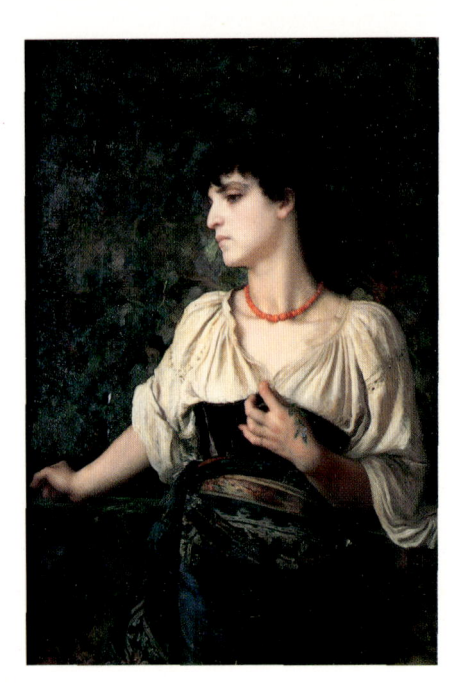

Ernest Hébert

Grenoble, 1817
La Tronche, 1908

Bibiana

1891
Oil on canvas
97 x 67
Gift of Mme Hébert, 1908

Ernest Hébert was, with Fantin-Latour, Grenoble's most famous 19th century painter. He was awarded the Grand Prix de Rome, and was twice director of the Académie de France in Rome. *Bibiana* was painted during his second stay in Italy. The palette, dominated by cold tones and a discreet chiaroscuro, together with the picturesque model and her restrained attitude, create a form of poetry very close to the Symbolist sensibility.

View of the Isère Valley from Saint Egrève

c. 1844
Oil on canvas
148 x 229
Presented by the State, 1844

Jean Achard

Voreppe, 1807
Grenoble, 1884

Achard, the founder of the Dauphiné school of painting, participated, together with Théodore Rousseau and Charles-François Daubigny, in the development of a modern school of landscape painting. He travelled throughout France, but his subjects were mainly taken from his region, and were executed in a style influenced by the Flemish masters. This vision of the countryside near Grenoble is characteristic of his art: peaceful composition in a succession of planes, where the mountains and rocks are made familiar by being bathed in the last light of day, with textures and relief being scrupulously respected. The sky, with the strangely-placed cloud and the dry tone gradation, helps us understand a remark made by the painter Eugène Boudin: "Old Achard couldn't paint the sky, he pretended this element didn't exist."

Laurent Guétal

Vienne, 1841
Grenoble, 1892

Eychauda Lake

1886
Oil on canvas
182 x 262
Acquired in 1886

With Jean Achard, Abbé Laurent Guétal was the most important painter of Dauphiné landscapes during the second half of the 19th century. *Eychauda Lake* is built in horizontal layers, starting in the foreground with rocks split by frost, then the lake, the mountain enclosing it, behind which the sun is setting, and finally the distant Oisans mountains, reflected in the metallic surface of the water, thus closing the landscape in upon itself. The absence of any human trace renders the setting all the more harsh and grandiose. The palette, dominated by coloured greys, is made velvety by the matt texture of the pigment. The reconstruction of the landscape makes it seem more imposing and absolute than it is in reality (and it is, in fact, so vast that it is impossible to see the mountains reflected in the lake); a careful observation of the light — warm both in the foreground and the background — has enabled the painter to unify the composition. The majesty of this work links Guétal's art to that of his contemporaries in American landscape painting, such as Frederick Edwin Church, who succeeded in marrying a feeling for detail with monumentality of form.

*The Vénéon Valley at
Saint Christophe en Oisans*

1894
Oil on canvas
200 x 320
Acquired in 1894

Charles Bertier

Grenoble, 1860-1924

Bertier, whose vocation had been encouraged by the Abbé Bertier and by Achard, is one of the main representatives of the Dauphiné school of painting. This landscape, whose sketch is also in the museum's collection, strikes immediately by its astonishing dimensions, especially when compared to the landscapes painted by the artists of the school of Barbizon. The immense panorama is entered by following the features of the mountains, plane after plane, as was usual with classical compositions. The realistic and scrupulous description of the subject is due to Bertier's conviction that he was helping to invent a new genre: Alpine landscape. Thus there is no human presence or effect of light to distract from the observation of the rough, stony or snowy paths, mountain streams, rocks and precipices: the *Vénéon Valley* is painted with topographic accuracy. Bertier's attitude meant that his work evolved very little with the years; a great number of his paintings were acquired by the museum, and, in 1922, he tried to stop Andry-Farcy, the new curator, from transforming it into a place showing avant-garde works.

Fantin-Latour is the greatest of the painters who were born in Grenoble. He first studied under his father, Jean-Théodore, and later in Paris, where he got to know Whistler and Manet, whose work he greatly admired; with these artists, and also Courbet, he belonged to the "Realist" group, whose principles are characterized by the absence of ornamentation shown in the *Portrait of Louise Riesener*. The model is the daughter of the painter Léon Riesener (1808-1878), a friend of Fantin-Latour and a cousin of Delacroix. The sobriety of the pose, the bold outline standing out against the neutral background, the use of light and shade to model the forms and enhance the face, the range of colours, reduced to a harmony of greys, and the hieratic pose of the sitter — all these elements contribute to the silence and poetry of the composition.

Portrait of Louise Riesener

1886
Oil on canvas
100 x 80
Bequest of Mme Escholier, 1969

90 Henri Fantin-Latour

Grenoble, 1836
Buré, 1904

Unlike the *Portrait of Louise Riesener*, which is almost a grisaille, this still life uses strong colours. The composition is of unequivocal simplicity: on a bare background divided into two planes of neutral colours, a beautiful blue-patterned vase filled with hyacinths and stock between a dish of strawberries and a glass of red wine. The forms are layered into two oblique lines, and the animated composition is strongly centred. This painting, with its brilliant harmony of colours, was given by Fantin-Latour to his fiancée, Victoria Dubourg, on the day of their engagement.

Still Life, also known as *"The Engagement"*

1869
Oil on canvas
32 x 29
Bequest of Mme Fantin-Latour, 1921

Ancient Art

Eugène Boudin

Honfleur, 1824
Deauville, 1898

Antwerp, the Harbour

1876
Oil on canvas
69 x 97
Loaned by the State in 1952

Painted two years after Boudin had been invited by the Impressionists, who considered him a precursor to their movement, to join their first exhibition, this view of the harbour at Antwerp belongs to the painter's mature period. The light, vibrant touch, and the camaïeu of ochres, are proof of the painter's extremely acute vision, as he set it down *in situ*, of water, sky, and the movement of air and light. "Float in the sky, attain the softness of the coast," this was Boudin's aspiration, which, as we know, contributed to Monet's realization that nature was in perpetual movement.

View of Montmartre from the Cité des Fleurs at Les Batignolles

1869
Oil on canvas
70 x 117
Gift of Mme Rousselin, 1901

Alfred Sisley

Paris, 1839
Moret sur Loing, 1899

This view of Montmartre (now the 18th arrondissement of Paris) was painted by Sisley at the beginning of his career. The broad panorama is divided into horizontal bands. The palette is limited to cold colours: green in the foreground, various tones of bluish-grey, with a few touches of pale ochre in the middle ground, and bluish-white for the sky. Every shape is sharply defined by Sisley's precise touch and his subtle colour gradations. The clarity of the construction and the precise technique show Sisley to be closer to the Barbizon school than to the Impressionist æsthetic vision. The only Impressionist exhibition in which he took part was that of 1874.

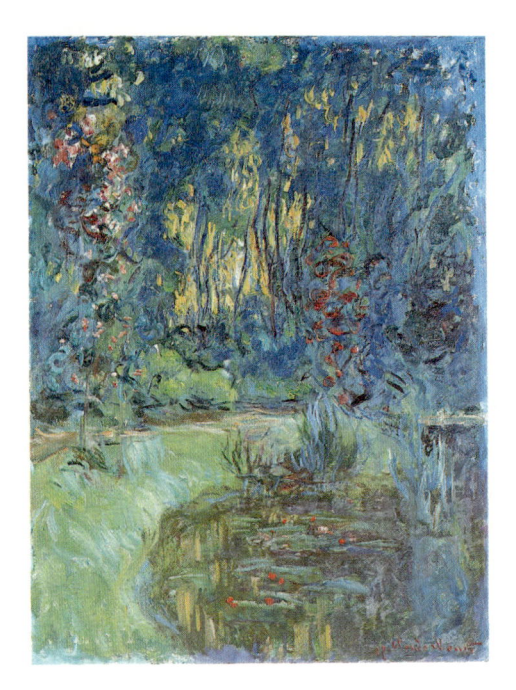

Claude Monet

Paris, 1840
Giverny, 1926

A Corner of the Pond at Giverny

1918-1919
Oil on canvas
117 x 83
Gift of the artist, 1923

In 1891, Monet began work on a "water garden" in his Giverny property, diverting the water of the Epte river to form a pond. The plants which grew on the banks and the surface of the still water, along with the light filtered by the foliage, are the subject of this work. Painted with long, quick brushstrokes, it gives the viewer little more than a coloured vibration, the masses and surfaces being disrupted by the free play of the painter's hand; and it is only from a distance that the organization and the meaning of the painting can be understood. This Dionysian landscape is a prefiguration of gestural painting. It was donated to the museum by Monet to "encourage it in its modernist tendencies."

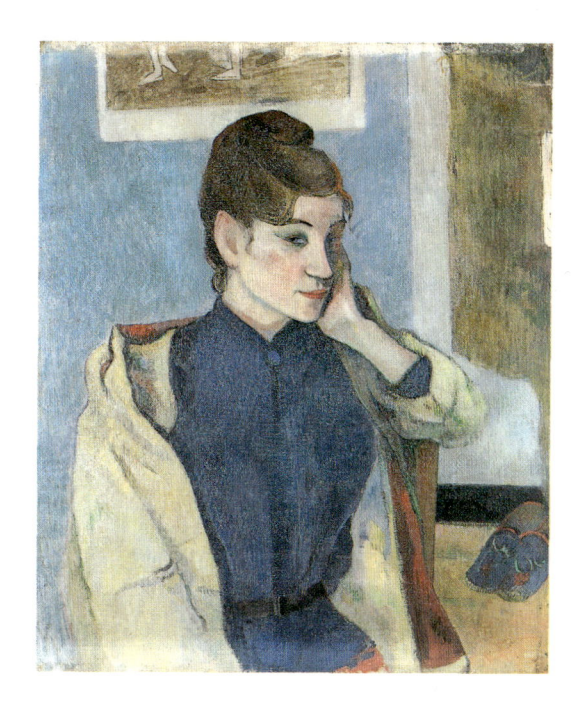

Portrait of Madeleine Bernard

1888
Oil on canvas
72 x 58
Acquired in 1923

Paul Gauguin

Paris, 1848
Atuana (Marquesas Islands), 1903

It was during Gauguin's second journey to the Brittany coast, at Pont Aven, accompanied by Émile Bernard and his sister Madeleine, that he painted the young woman's portrait. She is shown half-length, in a room adorned with a print by Jean-Louis Forain. Two double lines — a continuous vertical and a short horizontal, both on the right — define a space which has strong links with Japanese compositions, all the more so as the print is cut off by the edge of the painting. In this very rigid environment, a contrast is provided by the long, tense line enclosing the figure, and by the primary colours, which have been applied to the canvas in vertical brushstrokes, forming flat areas of paint without modulation, although certain parts of the body and the clothing are given a slight amount of volume. The unified treatment of the composition, drawing and colour define Gauguin's "syntheticism" — a desire for abstraction.

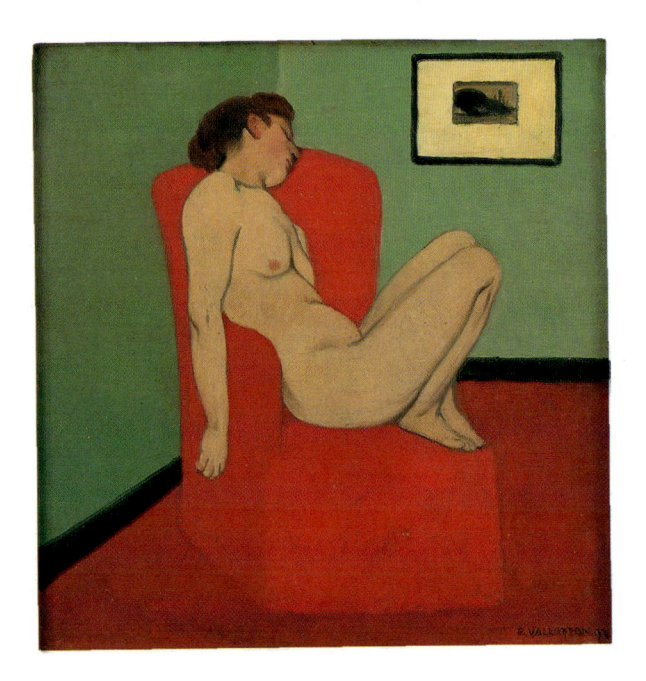

Felix Vallotton

Lausanne (Switzerland), 1865
Paris, 1925

Naked Woman Sitting in an Armchair

1897
Oil on canvas
30 x 29
Acquired in 1975

In 1897, Vallotton painted a number of nudes, with the collective title "Intimacy". The small format of the Grenoble painting immediately sets the tone of the series. A naked young woman is shown in profile, asleep, her head turned towards the back of the picture, legs folded on her armchair. The purposely reduced format, which excludes all superfluous detail, and the limited number of lines and colours, enable the sensitivity of the painter to gain great plastic power in the depiction of this tranquil scene. Vallotton did a lot of engravings, and this medium taught him the effectiveness of a simple opposition between black and white. This is the effect he re-creates here by opposing red and its complementary colour, as well as black and white, in juxtaposition and with similar tonal values, painted in large flat surfaces. This coloured schematic representation defines a closed space formed by three convergent planes, i.e. the vertical and horizontal edges which reflect the insertion of the nude body into a right angle, the stable figure formed by the passe-partout picture hanging on the wall, and the format of the painting itself (a slightly flattened square). With this painting, Vallotton's reflection on forms reaches an abstract level that prefigures Mondrian's art.

20th Century Art

Rooms 25 to 53

Paul Signac

Paris, 1863-1935

Saint Tropez, or *Le Sentier de Douane*

1905
Oil on canvas
72 x 92
Agutte-Sembat Bequest, 1923

Signac made frequent use of the landscape illustrated in this painting, the first version dating from 1902. The work shown here, executed the year Fauvism made its appearance, shows Signac's predilection for the Divisionist theory — as Pointillism was also called — based on the laws of optics as set out by Chevreul, Blanc and Rood: this theory recommended that, in order to properly transpose light and mark contrasts, the colours of the prism should be juxtaposed in separate brushstrokes, and not mixed on the palette; the eye would thus better perceive their brilliance through simultaneous contrasts, and would make the synthesis by itself. The small square or rectangular brushstrokes, regularly disposed, and orientated according to the lines of the composition, indicate the patiently worked-out technical mastery of the artist.

Still Life with Watermelon, Vases and Carpet

Oil on fibrocement
100 x 120
Agutte-Sembat Bequest, 1923

Georgette Agutte

Paris, 1867
Chamonix, 1922

This work was painted by Georgette Agutte, the wife of Marcel Sembat, who was a prominent politician during the Third Republic, as well as an art collector, critic and writer. He was also a friend of, among others, Signac and Matisse, whom he helped in their careers. With his wife, who was herself a talented painter and sculptor, he brought together, before the First World War, a collection which was to be the first French collection of Postimpressionists and Fauvists, including works by Signac, Cross, Rouault, Marquet, Camoin, Van Dongen, Derain, Vuillard, Vlaminck and, of course, Matisse. Marcel Sembat and Georgette Agutte died in an accident in 1922, and the major works in their collection were bequeathed to the Museum of Grenoble in 1923; Georgette Agutte had always kept her work in her studio, and the pieces in the museum's possession were chosen by Signac. The terms of the bequest stipulate that the collection (44 paintings, 24 drawings, 20 ceramics and 2 sculptures) should be exhibited in its entirety, and should be on show uninterruptedly for 99 years; this also applied to Georgette Agutte's works, which, after being transferred from the old to the new museum, were grouped together in one room of the new building, where they are shown to their best advantage.

If Georgette Agutte's sculpture, especially in the portraits, is of a realistic stamp, her paintings are much more modern, done in a style that was influenced by the Impressionists, the Nabis, and, naturally, by Matisse, as can readily be seen in *Still Life with Watermelon, Vases and Carpet*.

Henri Matisse

Le Cateau Cambrésis, 1869
Nice, 1954

Marguerite Reading

1906
Oil on canvas
65 x 80
Agutte-Sembat Bequest, 1923

This is a portrait of the artist's eldest daughter. Although her expression is meditative, she is in fact no more significant than the background. The painting is based on a contrast between two colours: red and green; the painter has covered the surface with these colours — both in opposition and with gradations — and then added another contrast. The basic tones are very strong — "one square centimetre of blue is not as blue as one square metre of the same blue" — and applied quite evenly. The gradations into white are applied with harmonious, graduated strokes for the wide collar, and more cloudy strokes for the background: the pleasure taken by the painter is obvious from the elegance, touch and subtlety of the tones. This work has a radiant presence, due to the brilliance of the colours, the balance of the composition — which is peaceful, as there are so few divisions — and the horizontal, rectangular format.

Pink Nude

1909
Oil on canvas
33 x 41
Agutte-Sembat Bequest, 1923

This small painting was done the year the Russian collector Shchukin commissioned *La Musique*. When Marcel Sembat saw it in 1913, he described it as "something unprecedented, which grasps you, something so new it alarms you," and whose true character is "the impossibility of isolating, with the eye, a single fragment [...] to the highest degree, insoluble and synthetic." It is, indeed, extraordinarily simple. There are few colours: the pink of the body, three blues (the azure of the sky, deep blue for the shadows on the ground, pale blue for the shadow of the body), and the green of the grass. The technique is restricted in scope, with flat surfaces and just a few oblique strokes of the brush, perfunctory anatomy and an expressionless face. There is no depth. Through this reduction in means, the painter gains a sort of imagistic literality so obvious and graceful that it induces in the viewer a feeling of serenity.

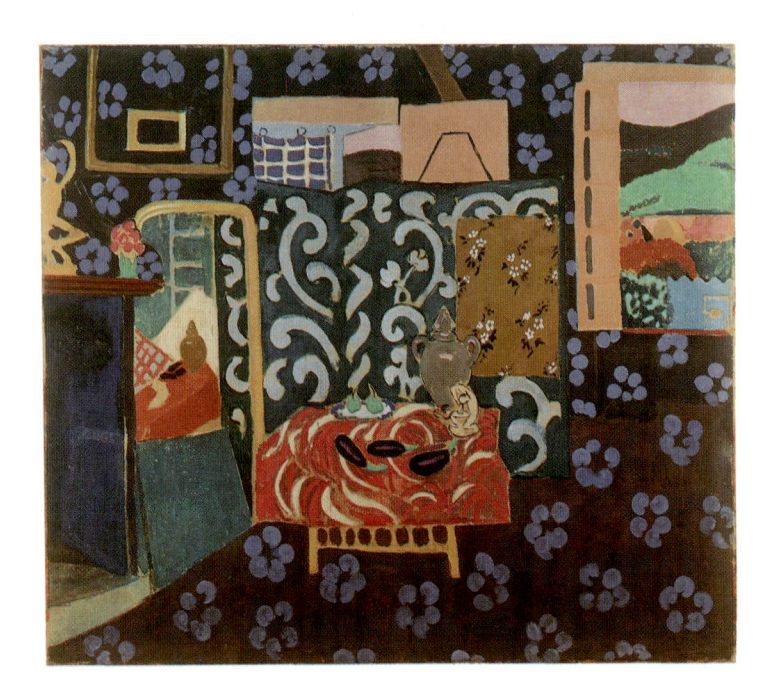

Interior with Aubergines

1911
Distemper on canvas
212 x 246
Gift of Mme Matisse
and Mlle Marguerite Matisse, 1922

This painting has had a prestigious career: the year it was painted, it was bought by Michael and Sarah Stein, and it subsequently came into the possession of the museum thanks to the generosity of the painter's family. It is the museum's most emblematic work, and is the only one of the four large "interiors" of 1911 which remains in France. This "decorative work", as Matisse called it, gives an overall view of a luxuriant surface on which blue patterns (flowers and short arabesques) are spread over a brown background. An order slowly emerges from this disorder through the juxtaposition of planes (the screen, the table, the mirrors, the open door, the window and the fireplace) which are so many paintings within the painting, stretched out along a diagonal.

The coloured vibration and flatness of the flowered carpet destroy the feeling of depth created by the diagonal which takes the viewer's eye beyond the "inserted" paintings. Matisse told Picasso: "I can astound the viewers without violence and at the same time stop them focusing, without their noticing it."

Colours are applied in large flat areas, but their thickness varies according to the brushstrokes, so that the colour of the support shows through in transparence and in unpainted areas, which increases the vibration. Strongly influenced by Eastern art (especially designs in Coptic fabric), Matisse first framed his composition with an edging painted in a flower pattern, but soon changed his mind: thus, the painting opens up into the space upon which it radiates, and appears to force the viewer into its universe.

The Cypresses at Cassis

1907
Oil on canvas
46 x 38
Agutte-Sembat Bequest, 1923

André Derain

Chatou, 1880
Garches, 1954

Derain always attempted to express shape in its totality, and took part, right from the start, in the creation of Fauvism. After 1907, he moved towards a stylization of shapes such as can readily be perceived in this painting. Here, in an almost flat space, he staggers surfaces rendered autonomous by the divisions of the lines surrounding them, at the same time that they are made interdependent by the colours, which are applied in broad layers. The brilliant colours of the first Fauvist paintings have disappeared, to be replaced by a more restricted palette; the paint is handled roughly, and gives a powerful sense of dramatic tension to this Mediterranean landscape.

Albert Marquet

Bordeaux, 1875
Paris, 1947

The Pont Saint-Michel

1910-1911
Oil on canvas
65 x 81
Agutte-Sembat Bequest, 1923

Marquet, as a native of Bordeaux, was particularly fond of painting landscapes with a river or harbour. The work shown here, which is certainly one of the most beautiful versions he painted of this particular scene, is a view of the Seine, probably seen from the window of the studio he had just taken over from Matisse. The composition is organized along horizontal lines — the black line in the water, the two sides of the road over the bridge, and the horizon — which reinforce the format. They are intersected by the two long curves of the river banks. The result is a calm, harmonious landscape, rendered immutable by the colour — a grey camaïeu, and yellows mixed with greens — while a picturesque note is added to this ordered view by the pedestrians, barouches and omnibuses.

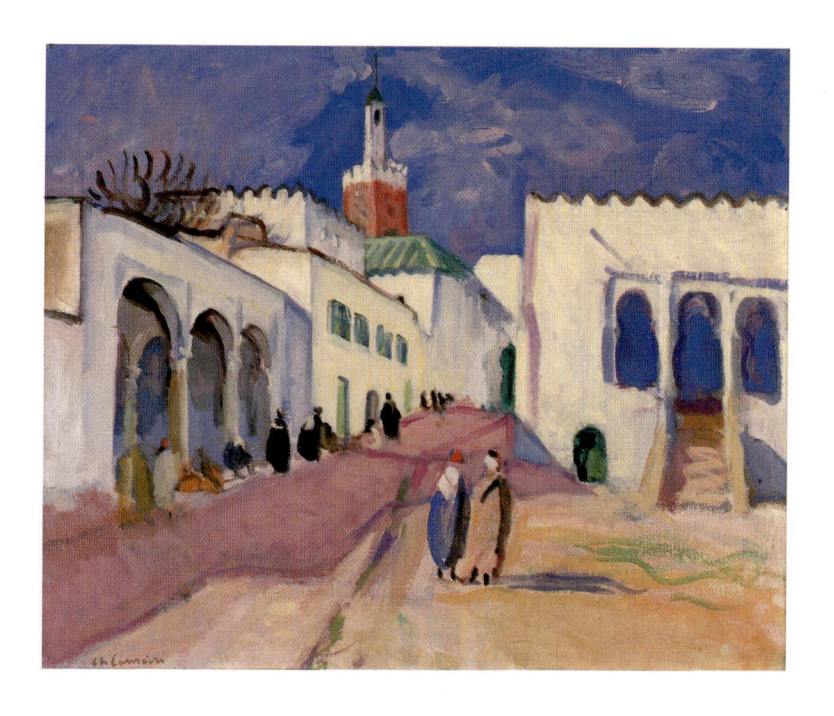

Tangier

1913
Oil on canvas
65 x 80
Agutte-Sembat Bequest, 1923

Charles Camoin

Marseille, 1879
Paris, 1965

Present in 1905 at the Salon d'Automne with Matisse and Marquet, who had been his friends since 1898, Camoin was one of the artists to whom the critics gave the name of "Fauves". This pretty view of a minaret in Tangier is characteristic of the way Fauvism opened up when it came into contact with the culture of Morocco, where Camoin went to join his two friends at the end of 1912. The construction remains Fauvist, with colour applied in large visible brushstrokes, but Camoin's palette is less violent, the black lines are thinner, and his touch has become broader and more fluid. White and transparent ultramarine dominate, in a perfect expression of the luminosity of the scene.

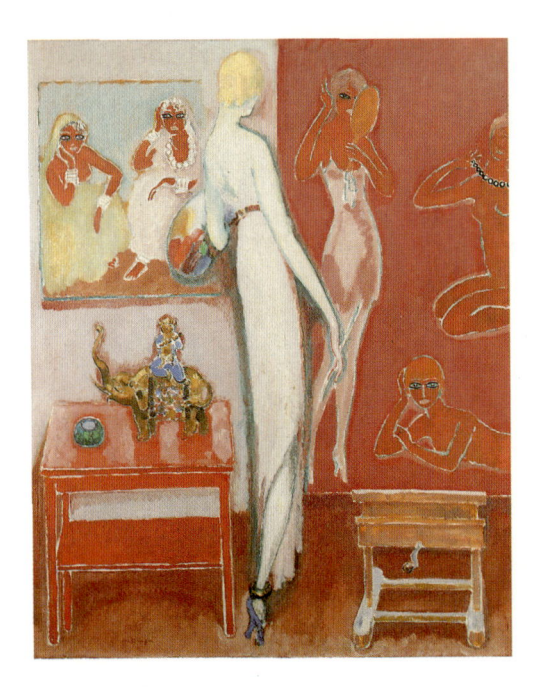

Kees Van Dongen

Delfshaven (Netherlands), 1877
Paris, 1968

Amusement

1914
Oil on canvas
100 x 82
Agutte-Sembat Bequest, 1923

Van Dongen exhibited two paintings at the 1905 Salon d'Automne, in the room called "La Cage aux Fauves". From the temerity of that period, the painting shown here seems to have retained the drawing style, but in such a pared-down form that only a play of lines remains, forming sign. It is clear, however, that the space built up by an imbrication of planes, the brown-red colour, reminiscent of Greek potteries, and, finally, the subject — the elegant, modern woman — announce the decorative experimentation of the twenties.

Chatou

1907
Oil on canvas
54 x 65
Agutte-Sembat Bequest, 1923

Maurice de Vlaminck

Paris, 1876
Reuil la Gadelière, 1958

Vlaminck, who was one of the first members of the Fauvist group, is possibly the only "Barbarian" of this exceedingly intellectual group; he did in fact give himself the name of "tendre barbare". The ardour with which Vlaminck has worked on his pictorial material, in a way that is strongly influenced by Van Gogh, as well as the amazing simplicity of a composition that places the boat right in the middle, are far from intellectual, although they did lead the artist towards the expressionism of the works he painted subsequently.

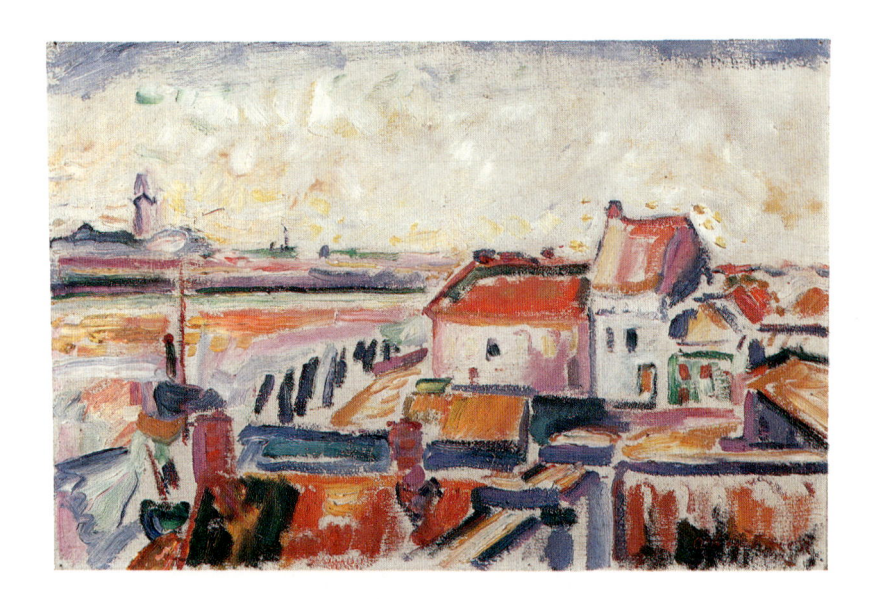

Émile Othon Friesz

Le Havre, 1879
Paris, 1949

Antwerp, the Harbour

1906
Oil on canvas
30 x 45
Agutte-Sembat Bequest, 1923

Painted after spending some weeks in Antwerp with George Braque, this is one of the best works in the series Friesz did of the harbour. He said he had wanted to "produce an equivalent of sunlight by using a technique of coloured orchestrations — passionate transpositions — based on the emotion brought on by contact with nature." This emotion is overwhelming here, with space transposed into a melodic, impulsive scansion of horizontal lines, in a palette where the dominant secondary colours are made to vibrate through the use of white interstices.

Guitar

1912
Oil on canvas
24 x 35
Gift of Marius de Zayas, 1941

George Braque

Argenteuil, 1882
Paris, 1963

This small grisaille painting is based on an architecture of planes which determine, by superimposition, lines of tension following two main directions, and lending balance to the resulting asymmetrical pattern. The fulcrum — the node where vertical and horizontal lines meet — is on the left of the composition, where it stabilizes the other, freer lines of the still life: a guitar, reduced to the curves of the sound hole and body, a sheet of music on which are drawn the close lines of a stave (or they might be the guitar strings), the oblique lines of a newspaper. The painter wanted only to represent structure; and it is with a similar economy of means that the chosen colour of the camaïeu has been reduced to an austere, and deliberately meagre, grey-brown. The treatment of the pictorial layer shows how the composition was sketched out in rapid brushstrokes, and the colour then applied in small touches, either opaque or transparent, to be finally engraved with the tip of the brush handle. *Guitar* is a statement about painting technique, i.e. the fact that composition, colour and texture are strongly interlinked; this represents a transition between the analytical and synthetic phases of Cubism, at a time when Braque, like Picasso, was reintroducing reality into his work in the form of letters and words; he reduced painting to a minimum of lines and surfaces, as a way of expressing objects and their situation in a space that was nothing more than the plane of the oval support.

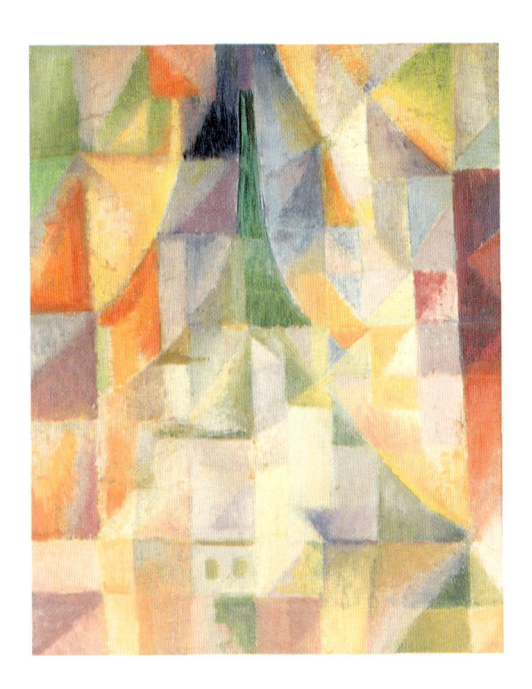

Robert Delaunay

The Window

Paris, 1885
Montpellier, 1941

1912
Oil on canvas, mounted on cardboard
45 x 37
Acquired in 1948

"Around 1912-1913, I thought of a way of painting which would, technically, consist only of colour and colour contrasts, but would develop over time and be perceived simultaneously and immediately. I used Chevreul's scientific term: simultaneous contrasts." This statement by Robert Delaunay, published in 1957 in *From Cubism to Abstract Art*, shows clearly how *The Window*, one of a series of thirteen paintings full of poetical and visual sensibility, was born out of a scientific approach. Delaunay used his knowledge of the law of simultaneous contrasts of colours, formulated in 1826 by the chemist Eugène Chevreul, to construct his paintings without using volume or linear drawing, thus avoiding the descriptive character of three-dimensional space and formal representation. The view of the Eiffel Tower through a window is more than just a pretext: its simple, geometrical shape is a symbol of the modern world.

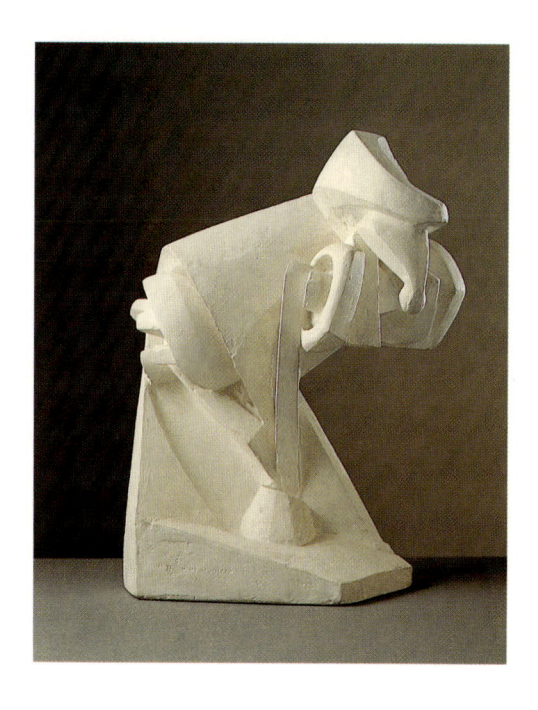

The Horse

1914
Plaster
44 x 42 x 24
Gift of Jacques Villon
and Marcel Duchamp, 1930

Raymond Duchamp-Villon

Deauville, 1876
Cannes, 1918

It was just before being mobilized that Duchamp-Villon started on his most important work, *The Horse*, which was to lead to *The Major Horse*. The plaster shown here was the culmination of a long series of preparatory studies (plaster, clay, drawings), and was used, after the death of the artist, to cast three larger-scale sculptures, of which the last was cast in 1984, in steel, in accordance with the artist's instructions. Duchamp-Villon shared the Italian Futurists' preoccupation with the representation of movement as a symbol of modern life; he had also studied, with his brothers Jacques Villon and Marcel Duchamp, the "chronophotographic" works of Étienne-Jules Marey, and had attempted a plastic synthesis of movement. The rearing horse is a symbol of the highly-strung power of the animal, assimilated to an engine. Using shapes which he simplified to make them analogous to stylized mechanical elements (axles, wheels), contrasting light and shade and seeking out lines of force, Duchamp-Villon made of *The Horse* a monument to power and speed, which were the major myths of the first quarter of our century.

Luigi Russolo

Portogruaro (Italy), 1885
Laveno (Switzerland), 1947

Plastic Synthesis of a Woman's Movements

1912
Oil on canvas
65 x 86
Gift of the artist, 1947

Russolo was interested in finding a plastic translation of movement and speed; with other painters, poets and sculptors he signed the *Manifesto of Futurist Painters* in 1909; he also studied Étienne-Jules Marey's chronophotographs, as Duchamp had done for *Nude descending a Staircase* (1911). The female figure in the centre of the composition is merely a pretext for illustrating dynamic sensations. The silhouette, seen in a sort of rhythmic multiplication of a single shape, is structured as a spiral movement which dissolves the forms. This tendency towards abstraction led to a more precise expression of speed, which, according to the Futurists, negates reality. The colour palette, restricted almost exclusively to shades of blue, does away with the third dimension of space.

Bottle of Rum

1916-1917
Polychrome wood and sheet metal
28.5 x 25.5 x 19
Acquired in 1954

Henri Laurens

Paris, 1885-1954

This rare construction — of the twenty-five similar works produced by Laurens, only three are to be found in French museums — is a good example of the renewal of sculpture brought about by Cubism, and of Laurens' originality in the Cubist movement. Here Laurens, like Picasso and Braque with their "papiers collés", put together diverse elements (wood blocks and sheet-iron, either painted or unpainted). The rigour of the composition does not give any indication as to the construction process, unlike the work of Picasso, who mixed real objects with fragments. And the external spaces are as important as the internal volumes. In a spiral movement around a vertical axis, *Bottle of Rum* offers the viewer, whatever his position, a delicate variety of shapes, colours and textures.

Marc Chagall

Vitebsk (Bielorussia), 1887
Saint Paul de Vence, 1985

The Cattle Merchant

1922-1923
Oil on canvas
99 x 180
Loaned by the Musée National
d'Art Moderne, 1990, Chagall donation

This is the second version of a composition whose first version, painted by Chagall in 1912 is now in the Kunstmuseum, Basel. The subject appears to be autobiographical: as Chagall explained in *My Life* (published in 1931), he had taken a cart to his uncle's farm to bring back some cattle. The frieze format, which gives a sense of grandeur to this peasant scene, is cleverly accentuated by the interplay of eyes and postures: the opposite movement of the woman carrying a calf on her shoulders, as well as the cow and the cart driver, along with the forward movement of the pregnant mare, create a tension that extends the scene beyond the edges of the canvas. The brilliant colours are unrealistic, with gradations influenced by Cubism. There are many different orders of size. The couple in the foreground, of whom only the heads and shoulders are visible, cancel all notion of perspective. The naïvety of the representation of space, which is close to that of medieval works, adds charm to the composition.

Portrait of Paul Poiret

1915
Oil on canvas
100 x 73
Acquired in 1934

André Derain

Chatou, 1880
Garches, 1954

This portrait of the celebrated couturier Paul Poiret was painted in August 1914 at Lisieux, where Derain and Poiret had been thrown together by the mobilization process. The painting has a strongly restrained, hieratic quality. From the Cubist heritage and his admiration for Cézanne, Derain retained a feeling for rigour and the simplification of forms, as well as a limitation of the chromatic range to light tones. The sitter is shown facing the viewer, on a central vertical axis, and is inscribed in a two-dimensional space. The treatment of the eyes, the rigidity of the body, and the back of the armchair, which evokes a canopy, reinforce the Byzantine abstractness of the composition. Poiret was very attached to this portrait, which, he felt, revealed his despotic, Venetian character; and it was with regret that he finally sold it, for financial reasons.

Alberto Magnelli

Florence (Italy), 1888
Meudon, 1971

The Café

1914
Oil on canvas
168 x 200
Gift of Mme Magnelli in 1974

The Café is one of the major compositions of a highly productive period in Magnelli's life; in 1914, in Paris, he met the major figures of the time (from Picasso and Apollinaire to De Chirico, Juan Gris and the Futurists), and this led him to develop a singular technique, half-way between abstraction and figuration. The elements shown here are drawn from reality — figures, chair, table, parasol, etc. — but are reduced to planes painted as flat surfaces, without gradations, in brilliant contrasting colours. The thin black edging of these planes creates a graphic network which gives the painting its unity. The juxtaposition of colour areas, whose outlines are for the most part composed of acute angles and curves, produces a syncopated rhythm which expresses the dynamism of the scene through a broad palette made up of pure, strong colours applied with great care.

Space Made Rhythmic According to the Plane

1920
Tempera on canvas
355 x 274
Gift of the artist, 1927

Albert Gleizes

Paris, 1881
Avignon, 1953

The beginning of the twenties was a turning point in the career of the Cubist painter Albert Gleizes: he evolved towards a technique dominated by flat surfaces and geometrical figures, as can be seen in this painting. Except for the four human figures, and the window patterns that resembles a New York cityscape, the painting has abandoned all links with reality, and the subject matter is the structure of the painting itself. Cut-out silhouettes with crisp outlines — contrasting angles and arcs — are juxtaposed along a dominant axis of symmetry. Each colour, each plane is related to another within the composition. Flat areas of paint fill the shapes with precision, and with great chromatic intensity; their matt quality is due to the tempera technique chosen by the artist. In this painting, Gleizes used all the dynamic possibilities of the planes, juggling with directions, rhythms and repetitions to create cadenzas.

Pablo Picasso

(Pablo Ruiz y Picasso)

Málaga (Spain), 1881
Mougins, 1973

Woman Reading

1920
Oil on canvas
100 x 81
Gift of the artist, 1921

Picasso did this portrait, whose model was the painter's wife Olga, after a trip to Italy in 1917, during which he meditated on the statuary of antiquity, as well as paintings of the Trecento and Quattrocento; this changed his entire outlook on style, and on the sources of his art. It is because Picasso placed equal value on these different forms of expression that this period was said to be a return to Classicism. There is the theme of the woman-statue; the contrasting pink volumes of the face and the hands, derived from the Trecento; the broad, reunified Cubist facets of the folds; the finger on the temple, taken from the *Portrait of Madame Moitessier* by Ingres, who was himself inspired by a painting from Herculaneum that he had seen in the Museum of Naples; the perfect drawing technique and the fondness for distortion (similar to Ingres and Puvis de Chavannes); the technique and the alfresco colour — these are not mere ornaments used to signal Picasso's cultural Pantagruelism; they are the characteristics of his art. If this work is so strongly poetical in expression, and at the same time a mixture of easily recognizable elements, it is because it gives the impression of a complete system of reciprocal relations between, on the one hand, Picasso's images and means of expression and, on the other hand, our culture itself.

Bottle, Pipe and Books

1918
Oil on canvas
73 x 60
Acquired in 1993

Amédée Ozenfant

Saint Quentin, 1886
Cannes, 1966

This is the first of Ozenfant's Purist pictures. It was painted the same year that the movement itself was created by Ozenfant and Charles-Édouard Jeanneret (later known as Le Corbusier). The Purist movement was to be a "general grammar of sensibility" for modern man. It advocated a composition system based on orthogonal diagrams, forms painted as a single surface, and strictly controlled drawing, colour range and technique, which would transform a painting into a "machine to move" the viewer. *Bottle, Pipe and Books* could have been used as a frontispiece for the book published by the Purists, *After Cubism*, since it follows most of their principles: the subject is a still life whose components, lighted from two directions, are reduced, together with their projected shadows, to diagrammatic forms; the choice of colours is an austere camaïeu of grey, slightly enhanced by white and red; the technique is exact and precise; the composition is synthetic and continuous, due to the scene being viewed from above. This painting symbolizes Ozenfant's search for a universal language.

Fernand Léger

Argentan, 1881
Gif sur Yvette, 1955

The Tugboat

1920
Oil on canvas
104 x 132
Acquired in 1928

The Tugboat, of which there is another version in the Musée National d'Art Moderne in Paris, celebrates the beauty of the machine in everyday life; this is a very different view from that of the Futurists, in the sense that Léger finds in industrial creation a repertoire of forms, a kind of "raw material" similar to the elements of a landscape or figures used by previous artists.

Composed on an orthogonal grid, the painting presents, in an interplay of contrasts, the analysis of the plastic elements of the machine and its environment: squares are opposed to circles, solids to empty space, flat surfaces to reliefs, colours to non-colours. This exploded, colourful vision of the world, reordered according to strict plastic rules, illustrates the energy of the machine and of human activity, to which it provides a cheerful, optimist equivalent. Humans, animals and plants are also submitted to a form of geometrical order; here, as was the case with the classical painters of the 17th century, Léger shows his belief in a harmonious universe.

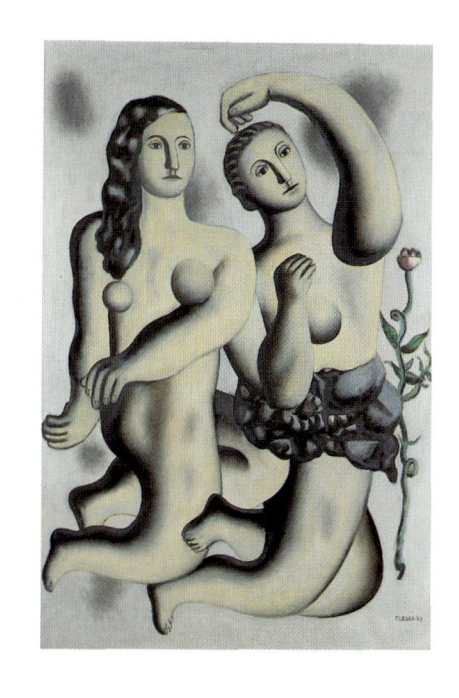

The Dance

1929
Oil on canvas
130 x 90
Loaned by the State in 1935

Coming immediately after the period of the large "Doric" figures, *The Dance* is one of the most beautiful example of Léger's "objects in space" period, during which he established plastic equivalents between subject and object. This painting shows two figures and a flower floating in space. The monumental proportions of the bodies are recomposed without any attempt at anatomical truth, while being twisted around a vertical axis: the heads are seen frontally, the chests in three-quarters profile, the hips in profile, the legs bent and foreshortened by perspective. The space behind the figures is devoid of depth, and contains only a few dense masses. One single vegetal element links with the natural world. The structure of the canvas, based on verticals and horizontals, freezes the composition, while the curves and countercurves of the bodies, the position of the limbs, and the lithe plant extending its sinuosities, all suggest flight. The palette is limited to greys: pale grey mixed with yellow or blue for the bodies and their shading, and an almost silvery grey for the background, expressing an intense white light, with no variations, although the volume of the bodies is suggested by the shading on the left.

The impossibility for painters to translate movement — Léger used the theme of dance in numerous works — is partially solved here by the close-up of two bodies frozen in movement — dancing and not dancing, weightless and heavy, graceful and hieratic — in an abstract space radiating light. The image thus created, monumental in scope and singularly poetic, takes on the value of a Pagan apotheosis.

Marcelle Cahn

Strasbourg, 1895
Neuilly, 1981

Abstract Composition,
or *The Washbasin*

1925
Oil on canvas
73 x 50
Acquired in 1987

Marcelle Cahn was a student of Fernand Léger and Amédée Ozenfant at the Académie Moderne in Paris, in 1920. In this painting she applies the basic principles of their teaching: a representation of the modern world by means of lines, forms and colours, with a constructive rigour reminiscent of technical and industrial civilization. The washbasin and all its elements, the tap with water gushing from it, the basin, the pipes, have all been stylized to produce geometrical shapes painted in bright, flat colours; the composition is based on horizontal and vertical lines on a flat surface. This is, indubitably, an *Abstract Composition*.

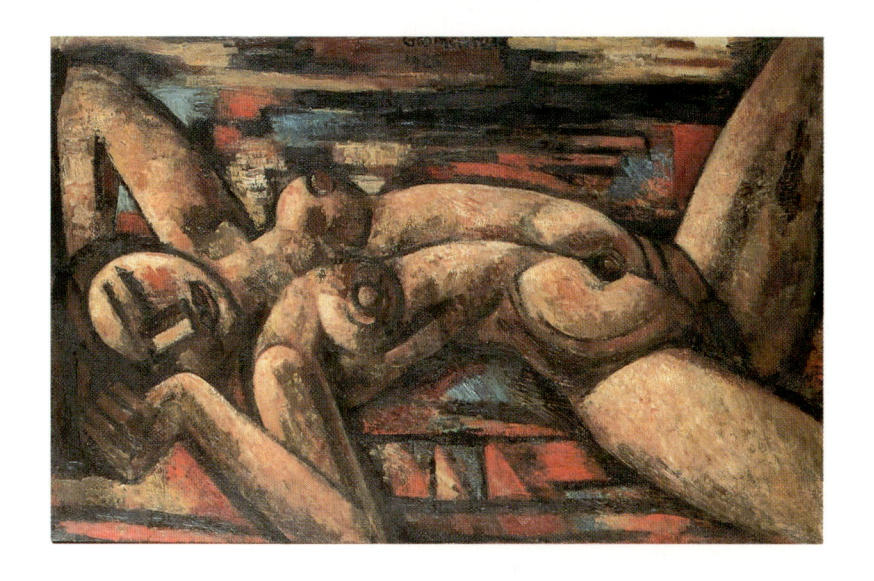

Nude on an Oriental Carpet

1926
Oil on canvas
65 x 100
Acquired in 1946

Marcel Gromaire

Noyelles sur Sambre, 1892
Paris, 1971

The female nude was one of Gromaire's favourite themes. This *Nude on an Oriental Carpet* shows a powerful syntheticism, and is reduced to angular volumes edged in shadow reminiscent of *Art Nègre* as well as Cubist construction. The almost monochrome palette is a mixture of deep reds, ochres and browns; the dappled brushstrokes express the robust sensuality of the model. The feeling for colour and the expressive realism of the work originate in the deep cultural links which Gromaire retained with his native region and the atmosphere of the North.

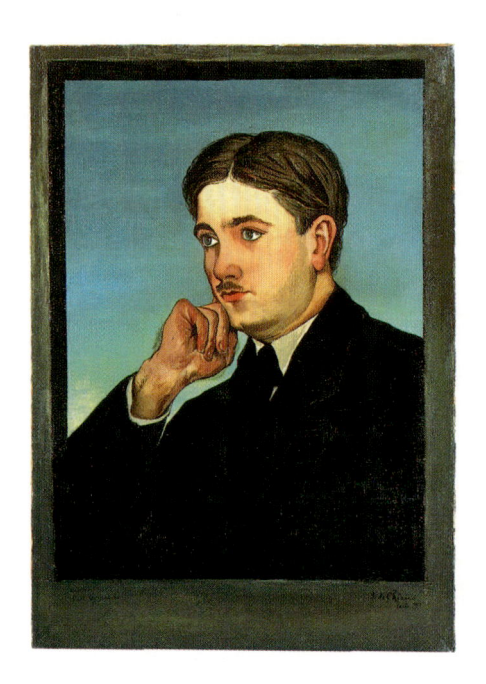

Giorgio De Chirico

Volos (Greece), 1888
Rome (Italy), 1978

Portrait of Paul Guillaume

1915
Oil on canvas
79 x 57
Gift of Dr Albert Barnes, 1935

Portraits are relatively rare in the work of De Chirico, one of the most influential artists of the 20th century, in whose figurative compositions — starting from 1912-1913, in the wake of Symbolism and the work of the Swiss painter Arnold Böcklin — representation was made to express a feeling of strangeness. This is a portrait of the art dealer and collector Paul Guillaume (1893-1934), who acted as an adviser, in particular, to Albert Barnes, the American collector who presented the work to the museum. Though little known, the painting is very characteristic of De Chirico's style, in that it shows his reverence for the art of the past: the composition of the psychological portrait is classical — the figure is shown half-length, in three-quarters profile, behind a window; the description of the face and hand is meticulous; the style is linear. The expressively-used light — soft around the shoulders, strong on the forehead — as well as the leaden colours and the neutral technique, are real inventions, as is the hieratic presentation of the sitter, shown in a slightly distorted perspective. This art of quotation avoids pastiche, and enables the artist to create an image of great plastic and poetic force.

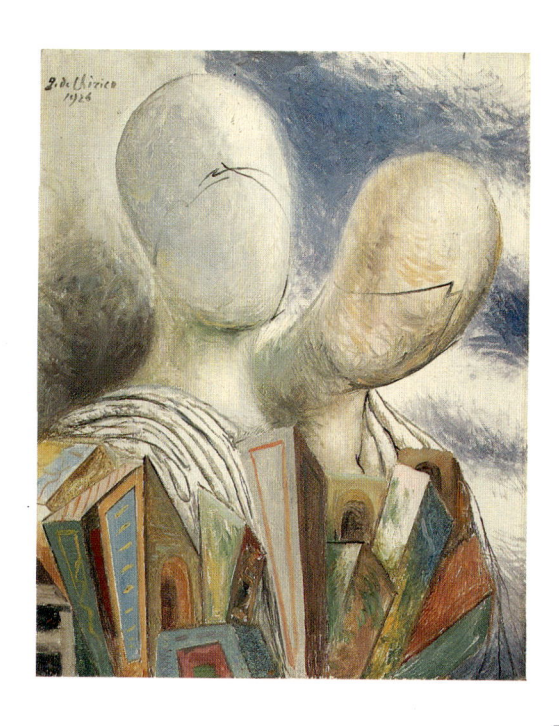

The Spouses

1926
Oil on canvas
60 x 50
Gift of Paul Guillaume, 1927

In 1915, De Chirico initiated "metaphysical" painting, whose key figure is the tailor's dummy; in this painting, the images of the two spouses has an astonishing introspective and imaginary dimension. They are united — with heads among the clouds made up of precise geometrical volumes — in a single bust constructed out of ancient and modern architectural elements, with classical draperies. One wonders what enables this couple to thus dominate the world with their serene, silent presence — is it the complexity of the cultural universe of which they are made, or the plenitude of their sentiments? The vigour and monumental character of the composition, along with the freedom and sureness of the technique, make this painting one of the important works by De Chirico, who, following the great classical thinkers, was bent on questioning the heritage of humanist culture and its relevance to our time.

Ossip Zadkine

Smolensk (Russia), 1890
Paris, 1967

Woman's Torso

1933
Granite
94 x 42 x 34
Acquired in 1933

It was in 1920 that Zadkine, an important Cubist sculptor, returned to direct cutting. The *Torso*, hewed out of a magnificent block of Burgundy granite, shows the artist's mastery of a technique which was rarely used at the time. The sculpture, imbued with a monumental statis, is steeped in the spirit of classical art, and more particularly the art of archaic Greece, as well as Michelangelo's statuary. Nevertheless, the flattened surfaces and concave contour lines belong to a Modernism that directly follows on from Cubist creations. This sculpture is a perfect example of the "return to order" which was felt throughout European art in the twenties, and yet does not in any way reject the modern urge to experiment.

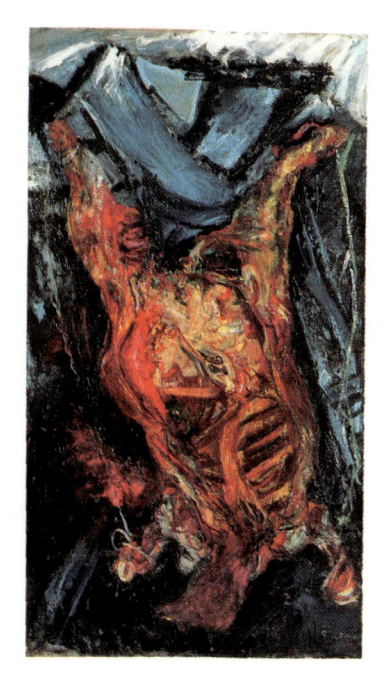

The Flayed Ox

1925
Oil on canvas
202 x 114
Acquired in 1932

Chaïm Soutine

Smilovichi (Lithuania), 1893
Paris, 1943

This is the most imposing of the variations done by Soutine on the theme of *The Flayed Ox,* painted by Rembrandt in 1655, and now in the Louvre. The naturalistic subject, melting into warm, golden tones, whose violence is subdued by the chiaroscuro technique, was used by the Dutch artist for a sublime transposition of the crucifixion. This religious dimension is absent from Soutine's work. The gaping appearance of the animal, whose shape has been brutally simplified without recourse to artificial composition, is the occasion for chromatic modulations of reds and yellows, which contrast with the cold tones of the background. The canvas is filled with the intensity of a struggle, physical as well as mental, against the paint itself. Thick brushstrokes, superpositions, dripping paint, hatchings and numerous corrections force the viewer into being implicated in this determination to give form and meaning to large splashes of pigment.

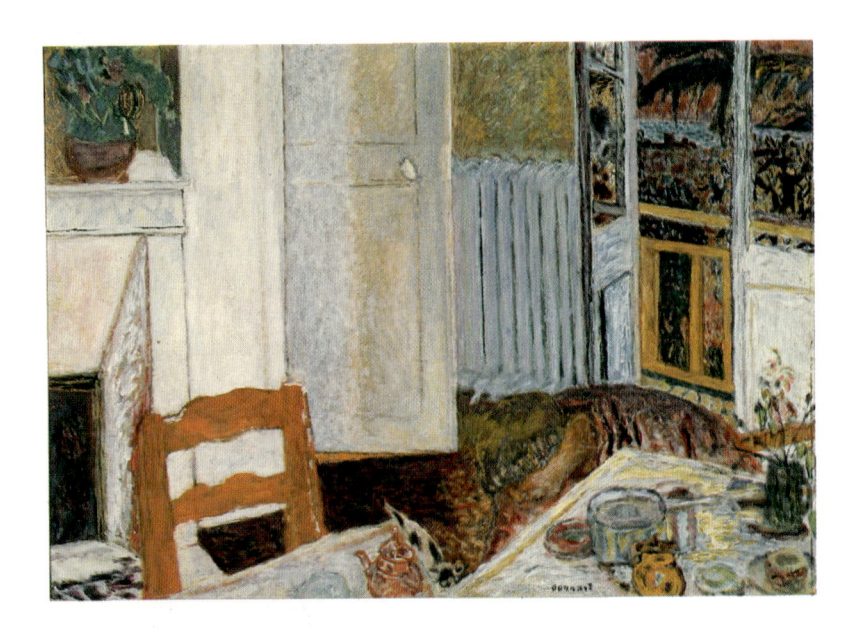

Pierre Bonnard

Fontenay aux Roses, 1867
Le Cannet, 1947

White Interior

1932
Oil on canvas
109 x 156.5
Acquired in 1933

White Interior is a perfect illustration of Bonnard's many innovations in layout, image structure, the translation of space and light, and in painting technique. The frame cuts brutally into the table, whose obtuse angle, from a raised perspective, forms two oblique lines that draw the viewer into the painting, while, on the contrary, the dynamic scansion of vertical lines and the interplay of planes invite the eye to traverse the image from the inside (the dining room) to the outside (the landscape). To this dynamism, as it is imposed on the eye, is added the vibration of the light, expressed in the way the colour and paint have been applied. The dominant tone, orange, used in a pure form on the chair, and then in many variations, plays with its complementary colour, also in a number of gradations.

White is given great intensity by pearly, iridescent brushstrokes of pinks, oranges and violet-blues. The colour-matter becomes so powerful that the viewer is forced to move back a few steps in order to distinguish between shapes that do not depend on their outline but on their luminous radiation.

Rue Saint Sulpice

1925
Oil on canvas
92 x 73
Acquired in 1982

Jules Flandrin

Corenc, 1871
Paris, 1947

While living in Paris, this painter, who was born in the Dauphiné, particularly liked painting street scenes in which the façades of the buildings led towards monuments. Instead of a detailed description of these buildings, Jules Flandrin preferred to illustrate the luminous variations, i.e. the changes brought about by the seasons and the time of day. Thus, in this view of the Rue Saint Sulpice, the composition is built up on colour contrasts between zones of light and shadow. The numerous tall, vertical lines of the buildings and the church which make up the painting, are echoed by the short, horizontal rays of light crossing Rue Saint Sulpice from the perpendicular streets. A few touches of colour enhance a palette made up essentially of delicate gradations of browns and ochres.

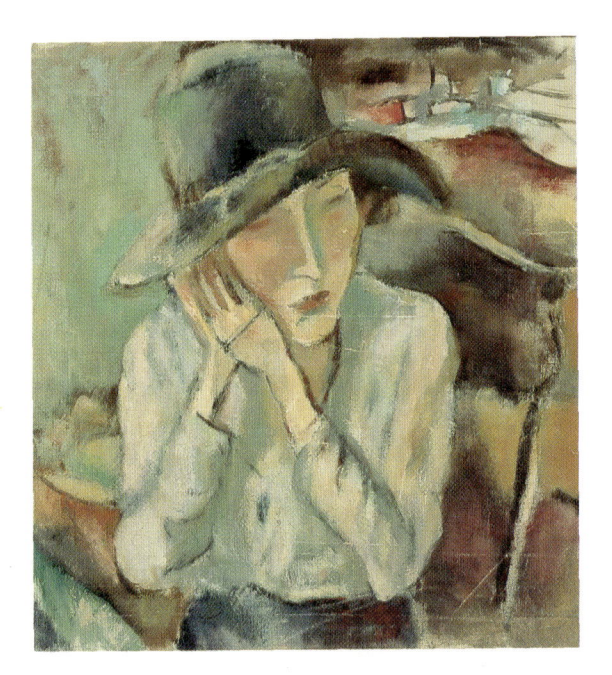

Jules Pascin

Vidin (Bulgaria), 1885
Paris, 1930

Hermine with a Broad Hat

1917
Oil on canvas
48 x 46
Gift of Hermine David
and Lucie Krohg, 1937

Pascin was a member of the School of Paris, together with Modigliani, Chagall and Soutine. In 1920 he began his elaboration of the "pearly" technique that is characteristic of his style. He used transparent pastel colours and halftones in harmonies of greys and ochres applied in such a way as to avoid thick layers, as well as shapes which were often blurred in the portraits and genre paintings and even the allegorical scenes, in an allusive, poetical or, at times, highly realist manner. Strongly marked by his debauched and excessive Bohemian life, Pascin's art reflected his way of life and preoccupations. *Hermine with a Broad Hat* was painted at the turning point between his first period and his newer technique: the drawing is still precise, but the subject is distorted in an Expressionist manner. The colours are close to those of the palette he was to use later.

Composition

1924
Oil on canvas
21.5 x 52
Acquired in 1970

Théo Van Doesburg

Utrecht (Netherlands), 1883
Davos (Switzerland), 1931

Van Doesburg was a painter, architect, poet and theoretician, as well as a founder of the magazine *De Stijl*. He painted this work the year of the German publication of his book, *Grundbegriffe der neuen gestaltenden Kunst* (Fundamental Principles of New Art Forms), in which he proclaimed his adherence to Mondrian's Neoplasticist principles. *Composition* is a non-figurative painting done in a neutral technique, with an asymmetric composition. It is made up of planes of primary colours (red and blue) and neutral colours (grey and white), separated by orthogonal black lines. Although strictly adhering to Mondrian's theories, and the reduction of formal language they advocated, this is a very personal work: the contrast between the thick black lines and the small size of the support, the narrow horizontal, rectangular format, and the small number of planes, give the work a brutal monumentality specific to Van Doesburg's work.

Bart Van der Leck

Utrecht (Netherlands), 1876
Blaricum (Netherlands), 1958

The Haymaker

1957-1958
Oil on canvas
140 x 140
Acquired in 1989

The Haymaker is one of the last works by this Dutch artist, who is almost unknown in France. Van der Leck, together with Mondrian and Théo Van Doesburg, founded the De Stijl movement, in 1918. He subsequently left the group to return to figuration, but did not give up the principles of planeness, primary colours and geometrical shapes. Thus *The Haymaker*, possibly a reminiscence of Millet and Van Gogh, is exclusively constructed from this elementary vocabulary of flat areas of red, blue and yellow on a white background. The composition is based on the long diagonal of the rake, which is composed of a yellow line doubled, in its lower part, by the red lines of a leg, while the second leg is made up of two flat masses of red. The other features of the body are stylized in the same manner. The choice of a square format and the abstraction of the forms standing out against a neutral background, despite a technique that does not conceal the corrections, make *The Haymaker* a strong universal image.

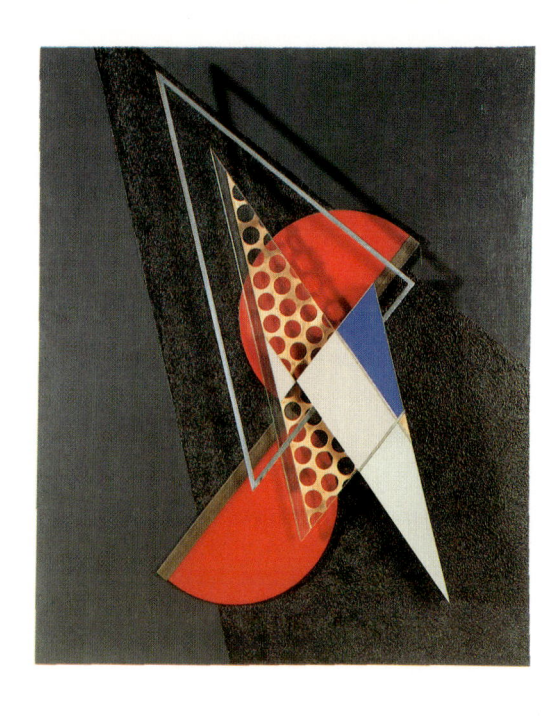

Relief N° 12A

1936
Wood, metal, plastic, Perspex
75 x 62 x 6
Acquired in 1993

César Domela

Amsterdam (Netherlands), 1900
Paris, 1992

César Domela was an abstract painter who took up the Neoplasticist principles of Mondrian and Théo Van Doesburg in 1924-1925. His evolution then became very rapid, with a dissociation of lines from coloured planes, colours being juxtaposed without any black edging to separate them, and the adoption of the oblique line; he then progressively abandoned painting, and started using highly diverse materials to create relief structures outside the traditional notion of the canvas. In his works, he experimented with plane and relief, line and surface, straight and curved lines, opaque and transparent areas, smooth and rough surfaces, shiny and dull textures, with constantly renewed invention. Domela's works were made with extreme care and technique, and the materials used were often precious; they are real "object-paintings". This is easy to see in *Relief N° 12A*, made in 1936, with its strongly defined geometrical shapes. The entire structure of the relief and the disposition of the shapes are subordinated to the oblique triangle. This choice led to an elaborate interplay of contrasts, which emphasizes the materials: transparent, smooth Perspex, perforated, shiny copper, and the matt-painted surfaces of the small triangles, reminiscent of Neoplasticism.

Jean Hélion

Couterne, 1904
Paris, 1987

Composition

1932
Oil on canvas
90 x 90
Acquired in 1993

When Jean Hélion started painting, around 1925, it was in a figurative style that evolved, from 1928 on, towards freer compositions where less importance was given to the subject. In the autumn of 1929, he met Théo Van Doesburg, with whom he worked on the magazine *Art Concret*. He abandoned Neoplasticism in 1932, but his paintings remained abstract until 1939, when he returned definitely to figuration. The 1932 *Composition* belongs to the end of Hélion's Neoplasticist period, though the work has retained some of the characteristics of Mondrian's principles, particularly the interplay of relations between elements, the absence of depth, the orthogonal composition, and the use of primary colours. But a certain freedom has been taken with this doctrine: no lines cross the canvas; the composition, based on asymmetry, is fragmented into four independent groups pushed to the sides of the painting, leaving an empty space in the centre. The black parallel lines, whose thickness varies with their length, and whose number follows an arithmetic progression, are associated with bars of red, blue, yellow and black. The dynamism of the composition, and even its baroque character, are structured by the position of these lines, which never intersect.

Graduated Sequence

1934
Oil on canvas
65 x 50
Acquired in 1969

Sophie Taeuber-Arp

Davos (Switzerland), 1889
Zurich (Switzerland), 1943

This work presents nothing more than white shapes drawn with precision on a uniform blue background. The alternation of straight lines and undulating curves delimiting the white shapes creates an optical vibration, one phase of a longer sequence continuing outside the painting, as can be seen from the last of the shapes, which is cut off by the lower edge of the support. *Graduated Sequence* was painted at the time Sophie Taeuber-Arp was a member of the Abstraction Création movement, and illustrates a very simple optical phenomenon created by the repetition by geometrical means of a form and colour contrast. Its self-evidence and simplicity convey a poetry full of sensitivity and harmony, the poetry which was already found in the Dadaist works created by Sophie Taeuber-Arp using noble techniques (painting, relief) and some that were more modest (tapestry, embroidery).

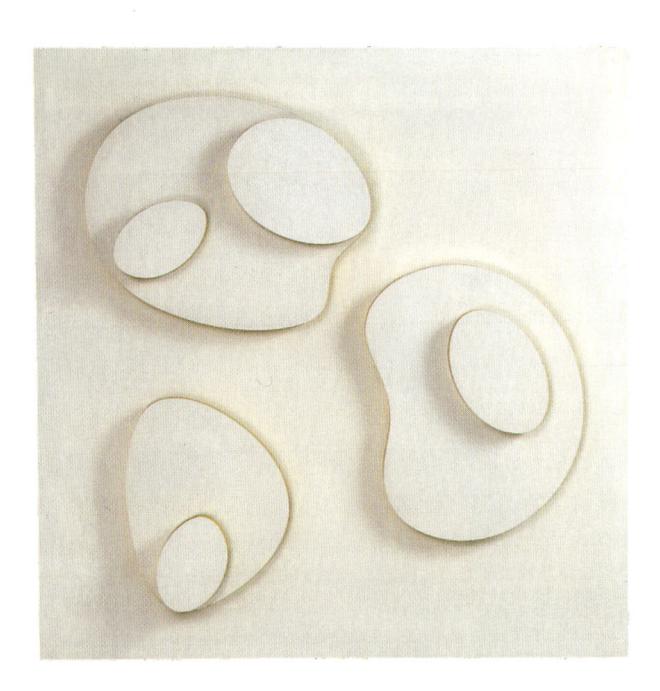

Jean Arp

Strasbourg, 1886
Basel (Switzerland), 1966

Heavenly Objects

1962
Painted wood
75 x 75 x 8
Gift of Marguerite Arp-Hagenbach, 1970

Jean Arp, who was married to the painter Sophie Taeuber, was one of the most important members of the Dadaist movement in Zurich. His first reliefs were done in 1914, and, from 1917 on, he created "terrestrial shapes" — irregular, organic and full of movement — an intricate blend of abstraction and nature, in whose spiritual values the artist found a source of comfort. *Celestial Objects*, the fourth version of this relief, was based on a 1958 collage. It is made up of "terrestrial shapes": three islets on two levels, placed on a square support. The whole relief is lacquered white, with the exception of the edges of the shapes, which are lacquered yellow. As the technique is totally neutral, the only variation in the light comes from the yellow-tinted shadows projected onto the white lacquer. A rare balance between poetical freedom and Constructive rigour gives this work a strong presence.

Sculpture

1921
Polychrome sculpted wood
53 x 36 x 32
Acquired in 1988

Auguste Herbin

Quiévy, 1882
Paris, 1960

Around 1918-1919, the painter Herbin, having abandoned Cubism at the culmination of a logical process, moved towards abstraction; he immediately became interested in sculpture and monumental decoration. In this 1921 sculpture, as in his polychrome wood reliefs of the same period, Herbin was attempting to achieve a synthesis between painting, sculpture and architecture. The interest of this research was to show how the treatment of a painted volume could be approached in a free and innovative way. The block of wood is sculpted and painted on four sides, a sort of totem placed on a black base. Each side is independent, yet linked to the adjacent sides by a common edge, and used as a frame for one of the four compositions. The colour distribution — black, red ochre and sienna, cut out of a white volume — does not yet belong to any specific code; it does nevertheless contribute, with a sober and restrained palette, to the creation of a rhythm that reinforces both the solid and the hollowed-out parts.

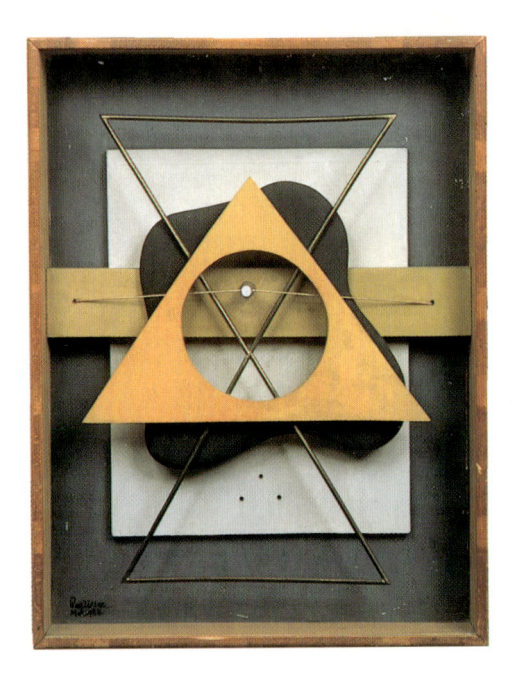

Jean Peyrissac

Cahors, 1895
Sorges par Savignax les Églises, 1974

Harlequin's Eye

1924
Wood, string and metal
48 x 37 x 6
Acquired in 1993

In a box, five simple shapes are laid on top of one another around a central axis (triangles opposed at their apexes; a shape cut out like petals; rectangles). These shapes, which are defined by their linear outlines or by their surface, are made of simple, varied materials. This assemblage, one of the first of this type to be created in France, resembles Constructivist works in that it is made of forms in relief where the dominant colours are greys and ochres. However, the title chosen by Peyrissac — *Harlequin's Eye* — slightly changes our outlook; it stresses the disparity of materials, and the central axis, which might represent a pupil; it also indicates that the artist, who occupies a place apart in the art of the period, was infused with a narrative and poetic intention.

Estructura en blanco   **Joaquín Torres-García**

1930
Relief in polychrome wood
53 x 36.5
Gift of the Fondation Abstraction
et Carré, 1987

Montevideo (Uruguay), 1874-1949

Torres-García was a Uruguayan artist who settled in Paris in 1924 and participated in the abstract art movement, though his work remained, for the most part, figurative. In 1930, with Michel Seuphor, he founded the magazine *Cercle et Carré*; this was also the year in which he made *Estructura en blanco* (Structure in White), which is in fact fairly similar to the work of Kurt Schwitters in its materials and crude appearance: roughly planed pieces of wood, painted white, nailed to a summarily painted plank. Although the composition appears to be abstract, and is reminiscent of Mondrian's work, it is nevertheless closer to the plastic universe of Torres-García — where shapes are positioned so as to resemble ideograms — in its simplicity, and because we are reminded of a figure. Torres-García returned to Uruguay in 1932, and became a prominent personality in South America, both as a painter and as a theoretician who helped to spread the ideas of abstraction.

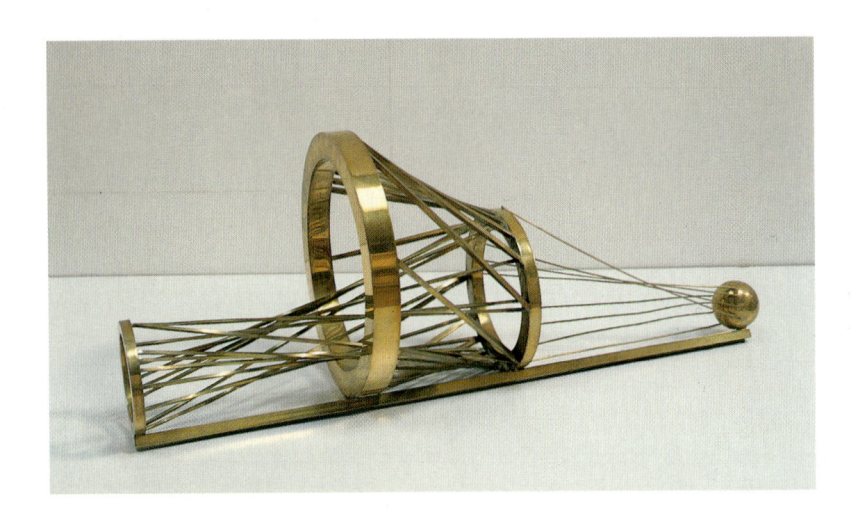

Anton Prinner

Budapest (Hungary), 1902
Paris, 1983

Copper Construction

1935
Yellow copper
50 x 50 x 135
Acquired in 1992

This sculpture, made by Anton Prinner (a woman who took on a man's name) in 1935, is the main work of this artist's "Constructivist" period. Prinner was at the time fascinated by the golden section, and mathematics in general. Constructed in metal like a machine, *Copper Construction* is close to being a "mathematical object". Three rings of different diameters and thicknesses are fixed on a horizontal bar resting on the ground. The smallest of these is at one extremity, while at the other there is a sphere which appears to be outside the structure. All these elements are joined by oblique bars of different thickness, which determine open volumes. This is a rare example of a sculpture by Prinner, whose career had its ups and downs, and whose destiny was a strange one. In this abstract work, with its harmoniously balanced masses, one might well see the symbolic image of a planet moving through the cosmos.

Linear Construction in Space N° 2

1949-1953
Perspex and nylon fibres
113 x 85 x 85
Acquired in 1972

Naum Gabo

Briansk (Russia), 1890
Waterbury, Connecticut, 1977

Hanging from a point between ceiling and floor, an array of lines describing surfaces spreads out into concave and convex corollas through which light passes freely. This construction negates volume as a stable, inert mass. In August 1920, Gabo and his brother Pevsner having been won over to Malevich's notion of an art without object, decided to use depth and transparence as a replacement for volume, and to look within the work of art for a "dynamic rhythm". This new vision of art tried to take into account the upheavals caused by the scientific revolution in the field of knowledge. Gabo's construction is indeed abstract, even if, for the modern viewer, it would appear to resemble forms revealed by scientific research. The superposition — through transparence — of its delicate textures marks out a changing space. The lines of force of the surfaces form knots then straighten out, generating "kinetic rhythms, essential forms of our perception of time" whose evocation has always been at the core of baroque creation.

The Wasp

1957
Wood
131 x 65 x 9
Gift of Ayin Béöthy
and Christine Dufour, 1987

Étienne Béöthy

Hèves (Hungary), 1897
Montrouge, 1961

Étienne Béöthy is one of the most important sculptors in the history of abstract art. In the wake of Brancusi and Archipenko, he founded his style on a working-out of proportions and the application of mathematics, using the study of morphology and the natural growth of forms. Every edge and volume of his sculptures was the result of systematic calculations based on a theory of numbers (those of the golden section). *The Wasp* is the finest piece in the Museum of Grenoble's collection of sculptures. The up and down strokes of Béöthy's three-dimensional tracery give a real motion to space, while the relations between edges and volumes directs the light onto either concave or convex surfaces in a masterful transposition of the links between time and space, the essential dimensions of life.

Composition N° 36

1937
Oil on wood
92 x 92 x 5.5
Gift of Mme Suzanne Gorin, 1989

Jean Gorin

Saint Émilien de Blain, 1899
Niort, 1981

When Jean Gorin, in 1930, produced his first relief, he showed himself to be one of the most gifted successors of Mondrian, for whom this type of expression was a means to go beyond easel painting and to synthesize all the arts in architecture. Neoplasticism, whose principles were laid down by Mondrian in 1917, is characterized by an exclusive use of vertical and horizontal lines, of primary colours and "non-colours" (white, black and grey) applied flatly on a two-dimensional support; his compositions were based on an "unbalanced balance", i.e. an absence of symmetry creating a rhythm through relations of contrast between the directions and sizes of the elements used, according to a rule which, inspired by a search for universal beauty, brought together ethics and æsthetics.
This 1937 relief shows clearly how

Jean Gorin, while remaining faithful to the spirit of Neoplasticist art, mastered a formal repertoire and a range of expressive possibilities which were personal to his art. Reliefs enabled him to approach painting in a subtle way, with the possibility of expressing lines and surfaces in three different manners. Here, the white circle stands out in relief against the square background in such a way that the composition, open and slightly out of balance due to a a fifteen-degree tilt, remains stable. The light tones, among which the blue dominates, give the classical elements of Neoplasticism a slightly mannered grace which is typical of Gorin's work.

Paul Klee

Münchenbuchsee (Switzerland), 1879
Muralto-Locarno (Switzerland), 1940

Landscape with Child

1923
Oil on wood
29 x 42
Gift of Daniel-Henry Kahnweiler, 1935

This painting was given to the museum by Daniel-Henry Kahnweiler, better known as Picasso's agent, and a champion of Cubism. He kept the frame chosen by Paul Klee himself. The violet inside edging exalts the dominant tone — a camaïeu of pinks, violets and blues, of which Paul Klee stated that it opened up a path towards the daydream. On this harmonic background a few signs have been drawn to describe a landscape with houses and trees, and a small child in the bottom left-hand corner. These signs resemble those made by small children. It should be noted that the drawings of children and insane people, as well as naïve and popular art, were "discovered" by Expressionism, and particularly by German artists. *Landscape with Child* is composed with great skill, and the signs are geometrical in shape: there are right-angled triangles for the roofs, orthogonal crosses inside the windows, etc. They are evenly distributed over the whole surface, and form a pattern of vertical strips.

The Forest

1927
Oil on canvas
81 x 100
Gift of the artist, 1931

Max Ernst

Brühl (Germany), 1891
Paris, 1976

Max Ernst was a major figure of Dadaism in Cologne, and then of Surrealism. In this painting we are invited to discover the image of a forest produced by frottage and scraping. This process is well known to children, and can be used to reveal the fibrous texture of a wooden plank, the line of a piece of string, or the complex surface of everyday objects: placed under a freshly painted canvas, they can be reproduced by scraping their raised shape with a knife, which removes the painted layer. In the present case, the blue sky and the sun were painted afterwards with a brush in order to give to the picture the meaning suggested by the title. The use of chance, either corrected or not, and of imagination — stimulated by the link between language and plastic forms — are characteristics of Surrealist creation. The forest theme, in the great tradition of German Romantic artists, is an important feature of Max Ernst's work. This painting is one of the elements of a long series started by the artist in 1925, and whose primary characteristic is the total absence of any form of life.

René Magritte

Lessines (Belgium), 1898
Brussels (Belgium), 1967

Wreckage of Shadow

1926
Oil on canvas
120 x 80
Gift of the Centaure Gallery
in Brussels, 1928

In this painting, whose elements are juxtaposed in the manner of a collage, five planes are shown at different depths and in various tones of grey; they define a desolate landscape with mountains. Verisimilitude is given to the landscape by the realistic shadows of the three objects in the foreground: a bird reduced to an eyeless head, a beak, a tail and the cylindrical rod holding it; a diamond-shaped frame containing a grid with four feathers; and a "tree" made of a cut-out plank in fake wood, placed vertically. The technique is cold and neutral (Magritte once worked for a wallpaper manufacturer), and the elements of the landscape are anchored in the real world through their illusionist appearance. Their interpretation, within the bounds defined by the title, calls for the viewer's participation in an ongoing interrogation on the discrepancy between visible reality and its pictorial representation. As a member of the Société du Mystère, which grouped together the Belgian Surrealists, starting from 1926 (the year *Wreckage of Shadow* was painted), Magritte was possibly the artist who did most to cast doubt on the validity of our belief in illusionist representation and, beyond this interrogation, to help us to renew the way we look at reality.

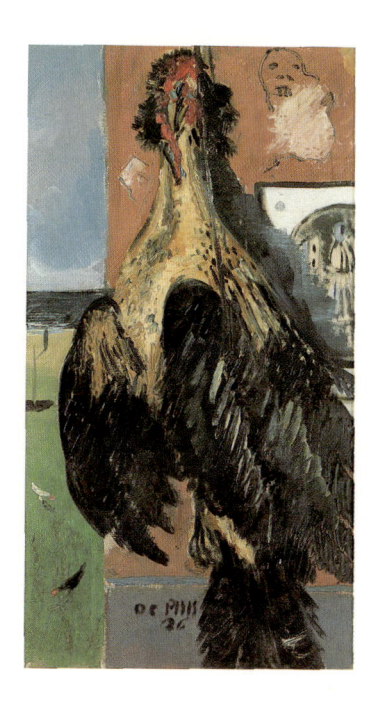

The Hanged Turkey

1926
Oil on canvas
80 x 45
Gift of Count Emmanuele Sarmiento, 1933

Filippo De Pisis

Ferrara (Italy), 1896
Milan (Italy), 1956

Filippo de Pisis was a painter and writer. He met Giorgio De Chirico and Alberto Savinio in 1916, and, later on, Carlo Carrà; he then followed their principles of "metaphysical" painting in a highly personal manner. The originality of his work resides partly in his choice of subjects, where he plays with incongruous parallels, or uses humanist themes derisively, partly in the nature of his compositions, where space is given preferential treatment by means of an often-exaggerated perspective, and partly in the violence (close to that of Expressionism) with which he rendered his themes, as can be seen in this painting, *The Hanged Turkey*, which he painted with a rich, relaxed technique.

Yves Tanguy

Paris, 1900
Woodbury, Connecticut, 1955

Nest of Amphioxi

1936
Oil on canvas
65 x 81
Gift of Peggy Guggenheim, 1954

The title of this painting affords an access to its representational world: the amphioxus is a small fishlike marine animal that lives hidden in the sand, and whose embryogenic development is similar to that of the vertebrates. This animal, which is as strange as its name, and whose morphology has been transformed by the artist, is shown here as being either slim or plump. In an empty setting without any landmarks, bathed in an unreal light, the animals appear to be petrified, outside time. There is a certain dryness in the execution of the work; the sea-like image might be due to Tanguy's Breton origin — his father was a sailor, and he had himself been a trainee helmsman in the merchant navy. He discovered Surrealism in 1922, and was particularly influenced by the works of De Chirico and Max Ernst; the principles of the movement, invigorated by his personality, brought strength and originality to Tanguy's work.

Navigation Series Box

1950
Wood, glass, paper, metal
34 x 47 x 11
Acquired in 1990

Joseph Cornell

Nyack, N. Y., 1903
New York, N. Y., 1972

Cornell worked on the "Cosmologies" series — to which this work belongs — more than on any other theme. Brought together here, in the closed space of a box — a metaphorical representation of the universe — are a map of the solar system, a child's ball, some rings and small stem glasses. The almost childlike symbolism of the elements, their preciousness and instability, and the extreme miniaturization of the space they evoke, lend a certain humorous charm to the work. Cornell's art found its final direction in 1931, after the artist had seen an exhibition of Max Ernst's collages, *La Femme 100 têtes*. His boxes constitute an original addition to Surrealism both through the themes they explore and because — given that the work and its showcase are the same object — they renew the language of plastic forms; they have also been constructed with great refinement: in this work the back of the box is covered with carefully aged printed paper, and the wood is tinted a magnificent amber colour.

Victor Brauner

Piatra Neamtz (Rumania), 1903
Paris, 1966

Woman with a Bird

1955
Oil on canvas
65 x 54
Bequest of Mme Jacqueline Victor Brauner, 1987

Steeped in images of popular art and old legends of fairies and vampires, the universe of Victor Brauner, who became a member of the Surrealist group in 1932, is peopled with fantasies and dreams, desire and terror. *Woman with a Bird*, with its bold black frame and pale background, illustrates one of the painter's favourite themes, in which a fantastical vision is linked to abstract symbolism through a simplified treatment of forms. The sober palette, the precise technique and the rigorous composition are characteristic of Brauner's final period.

Alberto Giacometti

Stampa (Switzerland), 1901
Coire (Switzerland), 1966

The Cage

1950
Bronze and painted figures
170 x 34 x 32
Acquired in 1952

The subject of this astonishing sculpture is a strange mixture of objects: a high stool, such as might be found in an artist's studio, on which is placed a cubical showcase — a cage — containing a bust and a figure on different scales, works within a work. Coming many years after Giacometti's Dadaist and Surrealist assemblages, his use of the traditional technique of bronze casting, as well as roughed-out, seemingly unfinished forms, gives meaning to this "sculpture-object". Giacometti's work is close to the Existentialist school of thought based on Jean-Paul Sartre's writing of the period after the Second World War: the artist is attempting to express the strangeness and depth of the links between human beings, as well as their links with the world, embodied in objects.
The Cage illustrates the way that man and artist perceive in the world a constantly shifting meaning; it is also, because of the impossibility of attaining that meaning, a metaphor of imprisonment, of individuals locked within themselves. In 1950, Giacometti produced a number of other works based on the same idea, such as *Four Figures on a Plinth*; but the emphasis given here to a more traditionalist representation of a figure on its own is a distinguishing feature of *The Cage*.

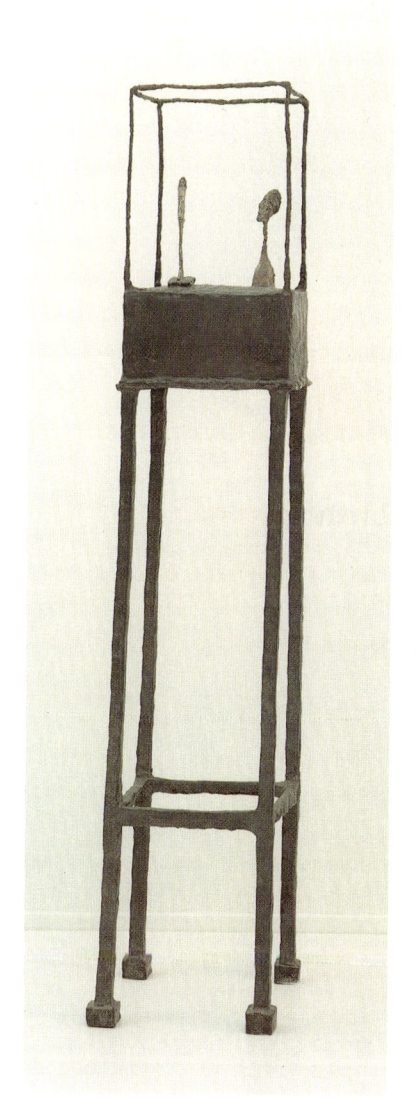

Balthus
(Balthazar Klossowski de Rola)

Paris, 1908

Young Girl at her Toilet

1952-1953
Oil on canvas
152 x 85
Gift of Mme Henriette Gomes, 1988

This painting is a fine example of Balthus' fondness for what has been called "intimist eroticism", as can be seen in numerous works dating from 1940 on. A young girl is shown naked, lit by the reddish glow of a sunset. The vertical lines of her massive silhouette, seen frontally, take up the whole height of the painting, and are echoed by the vertical edge of the piece of furniture on her left. In this stark composition, nothing distracts from the model and her closed face. The use of a matt, gritty paint surface, reminiscent of medieval frescoes and cave paintings, emphasizes the hieratic appearance of the figure. The formal and technical components of this work give an image of the young girl that is free of the ambiguous character of many of Balthus' paintings.

Street in Berlin

1931
Oil on canvas
93 x 141
Gift of the artist, 1935

George Grosz

Berlin (Germany), 1893-1959

Street scenes were often illustrated by Futurist and Expressionist artists, and many are to be found in the work of George Grosz, one of the leading figures of Dadaism in Berlin, and later a radical member of the Neue Sachlichkeit (New Objectivity) movement. For Grosz, it was in the streets that the corruption and decadence of modern society and large cities — Berlin being the epitome of turpitude — could be seen. This painting is held up to us like a mirror in which we are shown to be ugly, ill and false — especially women, as in the Celestine nun as black as death, the coquette whose shoulders are wrapped in a fur similar to Renoir's "*chienne*", with her stupid pig-like face, and the dry puppet figure. The unified representational space is painted a uniform earth-brown colour, and is invaded by a kind of "dripping", rough shapes sketched in colours applied with a dry brush. Each figure seems to have a life of its own, and to have no links with any others; in this painting, all representations, whether of objects or of humans, are equivalent. This moralist approach gains strength from a skillful composition and a rapid, vibrant technique with a highly expressive colour range.

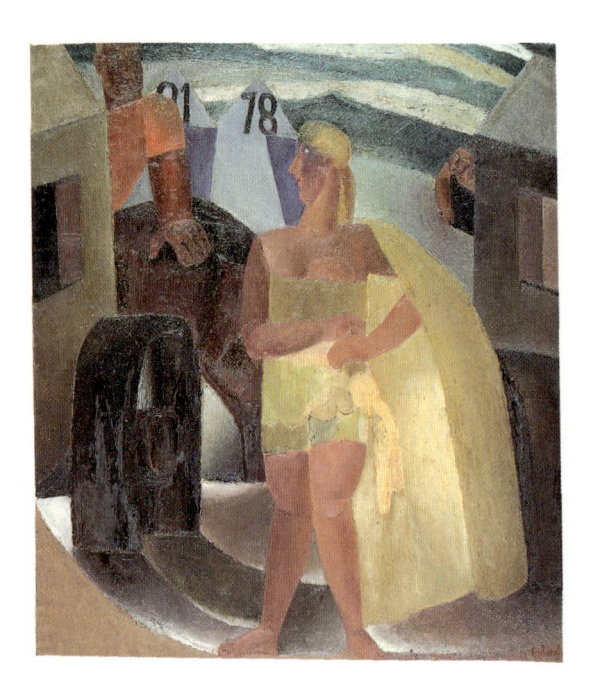

Frits van den Berghe

Ghent (Belgium), 1883-1939

Woman Bathing

Oil on canvas
110.5 x 96
Gift of van Hecke Norine, 1928

Frits van den Berghe was a member of the artists' colony of Laethem Saint Martin in Belgium from 1904 to 1914. He was influenced by Fauvism and German Expressionism, as well as by Cubism, which he got to know in Amsterdam in 1914. In 1922, he found a personal mode of expression: stylized forms, dull colours, solidly constructed compositions, subjects that were often close to the fantastical. This painting shows a Cubist influence in the way forms and space are treated. The subject — a transposition of the story of Susanna and the Elders — is treated in an everyday manner: a woman adjusts her bathing costume on the beach, while two men look on. The composition, the absence of depth, the simplified shapes, the palette — dominated by earth, ochre and grey — give depth and solidity to the scene, as well as a genuine monumental quality.

Circus III

1924
Oil on canvas
130 x 94
Gift of van Hecke Norine, 1928

Gustave De Smet

Ghent (Belgium), 1877
Deurle sur Lys (Belgium), 1943

Gustave De Smet discovered German Expressionism and the Cubist movement in Amsterdam, where he took refuge during the First World War. This work was permanently influenced by these two movements, though from 1919 on he used more defined shapes and less sombre colours. *Circus III* incorporates Expressionism, as well as Léger's Cubism. The Expressionists often used the theme of the circus, which, in this work, De Smet shows to be more stifling and mechanical than joyful: it is a two-tiered composition which opposes the lightness of the circus rider to the weightiness of the clown, with a palette dominated by warm colours (ochres, red-ochres and off-white). Léger's Cubist discipline has also been assimilated: the clown — made up of tubular shapes shown not so much by their volume as by their facets — appears as a laughable marionette lacking humanity. The way he is represented also refers to the naïve, childlike images "discovered" by the Expressionists.

André Bauchant

Resting by the Side of the Road

Château Renault, 1873
Montoire sur le Loir, 1958

1932
Oil on canvas
54 x 80
Acquired in 1947

André Bauchant, who worked a nursery gardener, is one of the best-known naïve artists. His work was appreciated and promoted by Ozenfant, Le Corbusier and Lipchitz. This painting illustrates the Touraine region, of which he was very fond; the landscape is composed of valleys, cliffs, fields and woods traversed by a winding road; the clouds above it are of a pink colour. This painting, in a technique which is both meticulous and rough, includes a plastic delight: the two farmers sitting back to back in the foreground, alone, silent, their hands at rest, next to a basket of red fruits. André Bauchant, the "peasant-poet", constructed his scene without any depth, with forms piled up on top of each other. The clumsiness and naïvety of the whole landscape contribute to lending it a certain grandeur.

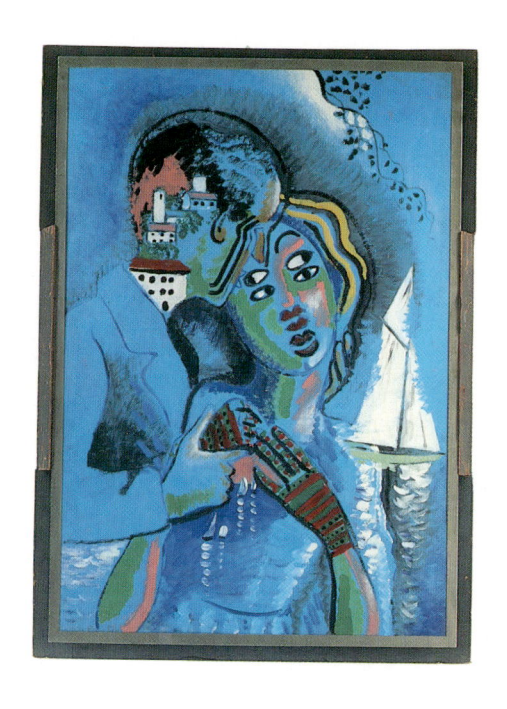

Idyll

1927
Oil on cardboard
106 x 76
Gift of Jacques Doucet, 1931

Francis Picabia

Paris, 1879-1953

Idyll was painted during a trip that Picabia made to Mougins; two lovers are shown embracing, transparent against an azure background on which are depicted, without any apparent logic, marine elements, mountains and houses. The faces are transformed by multiple mouths, eyes looking in all directions, and double outlines. With such textual and formal juxtapositions, Picabia was challenging good taste, and art itself, much more than in the collages of his Dadaist works. Collage was a medium which belonged to a certain avant-garde — in *Idyll*, Picabia returned to a traditional painting technique, which he treated with great casualness, and with gaudy colours, to create a provocative image that is a satire of a normally tasteful subject. The frame was made by Pierre Legrain, a famous decorator and book binder of the twenties.

Jean Fautrier

Paris, 1898
Châtenoy Malabry, 1964

The Fish

1927
Oil on canvas
54 x 65
Acquired in 1930

This painting is part of a series of still lifes in which Fautrier experimented with new formal techniques. The paint he used was light, almost transparent at the edges, but a little thicker for the fish, whose outlines are emphasized by a shallow, scraped line. Blue and yellow tones alternate with greys and blacks, and suggest zones of light and shadow as well as the palpitation and movement of the fish. The modesty of the subject, the strong colour, and the mastery of the texture achieved by a sharp drawing technique, show that Fautrier wanted to take on pictorial creation by a direct approach to the subject, and was out of step with the avant-garde movements of his time.

The Great Scythe

c. 1937
Wrought bronze
46 x 23 x 10
Acquired in 1985

Julio González

Barcelona (Spain), 1876
Arcueil, 1942

This work was a project for a sculpture that González intended to create for the Spanish pavilion of the 1937 International Exhibition, where it was to be shown alongside Picasso's *Guernica*, but which he was unable to carry through. The silhouette of a peasant woman with a scythe, standing on a small stone base, can be recognized in stylized form. This is, in fact, a more abstract representation of peasant resistance against Franco than *Montserrat* (Amsterdam, Stedelijk Museum), another sculpture by González. The brutal use of metal and aggressive cut-out shapes, the art of transparence and sense of space, give great expressive power to the work. The forms created for this "realist socialist" subject, as well as the construction technique, place González at the beginning of a true revolution in the art of sculpture — *The Great Scythe* is one of the museum's major possessions.

Camille Graeser

Geneva (Switzerland), 1892
Zurich (Switzerland), 1980

Kolor sinfonik

1947-1951
Oil on canvas
48 x 120
Acquired in 1987

Camille Graeser was one of the leading figures of the Zurich Concrete Art movement, which defined creation as the implementation of a precise, neutral technique in a rational system that was meant to rule the choice and relations of geometrical shapes and colours within a given space, while rejecting any kind of illusionism. In *Kolor sinfonik*, which is reminiscent of the work done by Mondrian in New York, the elements of the composition, equal numbers of squares in the two halves of the painting, are distributed over an orthogonal grid, and, for each colour, joined by oblique strips which do not intersect. The rhythmic balance is meant to recall music (as is indicated by the title). The painting was executed with an amazingly precise finish; the rhythm created by the oblique lines, the brilliance of the colours and the format produce a harmony of rare quality.

Six Rows of Systematic Vertical Colours

1950-1972
Acrylic on canvas
150 x 150
Acquired in 1987

Richard Paul Lohse

Zurich (Switzerland), 1902-1988

Lohse was one of the most rigorous practitioners of the Zurich Concrete Art movement. His aim was to justify all forms of creation through a rational system, and to give to an art liberated from subjectivity a role in the evolution of society. From 1943 on, after analyzing the works of Piet Mondrian, Théo Van Doesburg and Josef Albers, he adopted a course of action based solely on horizontal and vertical elements. The forms used (straight lines, squares and their multiples, always neutral and anonymous) are placed on a plane surface: they structure the whole pictorial field without creating patterns. The colours have been chosen according to a rigorous principle, without recourse to sensibility, and applied in flat areas. The composition, which is entirely programmed, quantifies colours and shapes. And indeed the work is a visual realization of the system indicated in the title. The three primary colours and their complementary colours are placed in such a way that they are never diagonally tangential, nor present twice in the same horizontal or vertical row. The succession of colours in the vertical rows is always programmed in the same way, with a displacement of two squares for each successive row. Lohse's compositions were carefully prepared with coloured pencils, and led to a number of variations. The painting in the museum's possession is one of the versions of a composition created in 1950.

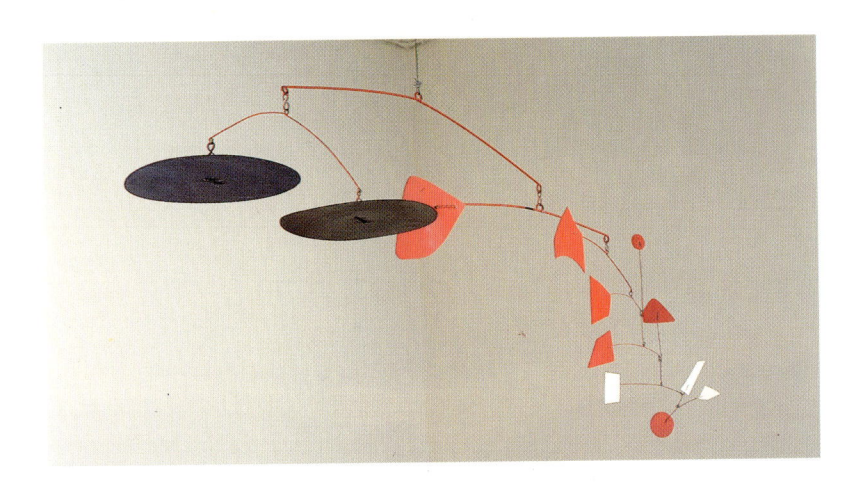

Alexander Calder

Philadelphia, Pennsylvania, 1898
New York, N. Y., 1976

Mobile

1970
Painted Metal
95 x 303
Gift of the artist, 1970

Invented by Calder in 1933 as a new way of looking at sculpture, works of this type were given the name "mobiles" by Marcel Duchamp. The one in the Museum of Grenoble, which is small, fragile and light, was designed to be hung in an interior space. Made of metal rods and painted sheets of metal, the mobile's equilibrium constantly shifts with the movement of the air. The slight motion of its elements creates random configurations which, together with the movement of the viewer, modify the whole space of the room. It was in 1930, after a visit to Mondrian's Parisian studio, that Calder's art changed drastically: from Mondrian he took the notion of abstract art, the systematic reduction of the components of art, and the constructive use of colour; to these he added the new dimension of space-time produced by real movement. This innovation, which was to be of great importance for the history of sculpture, added a poetical dimension to the discoveries of Gabo in 1920 and of Moholy-Nagy a little later — forms set in motion by the use of electric motors.

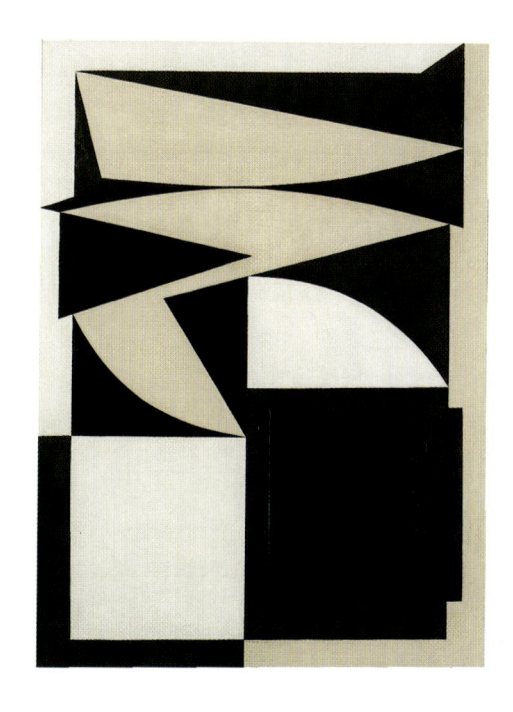

Zante

1949
Oil on hardboard
131 x 97
Acquired in 1972

Victor Vasarely

Pécs (Hungary), 1908

A series of colours chosen from an austere range, leading to a contrast of values interacting with simple geometrical shapes, the whole composed in a way that suggests the term "shape-colour": such is the challenge that Vasarely set himself in this painting, where the originality of his art stands out clearly. Until 1940, the work of this Hungarian artist, who studied in Budapest, was essentially based on black and white graphic compositions. *Zante* — one of the links of an ongoing, rigorous approach to the elaboration of an abstract art based on construction — belongs to the "Crystal" period, inspired by the village of Gordes in the south of France.

Berto Lardera

La Spezia (Italy), 1911
Paris, 1989

Dramatic Occasion II

1952
Iron
210 x 117 x 115.8
Acquired in 1991

This sculpture, whose volume results from a concatenation of different planes in a rigorous contrast of vertical and horizontal directions, establishes subtle, mutually expanding relationships between the large hollows cut out of the planes and the solid, opaque, heavy surfaces, between the curves of the cuts and the orthogonality of the assemblage, between the smooth and the rough. Beyond this highly abstract formal technique, the dramatic nature of the title manifests itself in the empty space apparently held together by the ascending curves, and in the brutal iron-working technique that can be seen in the cut and welded parts. This experimentation in expression was characteristic of the School of Paris, of which Berto Lardera was a leading representative.

Sienese Head

1960
Bronze
30 x 22 x 19
Acquired in 1964

Émile Gilioli

Paris, 1911-1977

Gilioli was one of the most important abstract sculptors of the sixties. Brancusi's influence can be detected in all of his work, and especially in the abstraction of *Sienese Head*. The ovoid form which springs out of the material remains extremely concentrated, and the artist, by refining the volume, has brought out the essential lines of the pattern. The only ruptures in this form, which is dense, closed on itself, are due to the interplay — the curved edges — between concave and convex facets. The purity of the lines and the perfection of the volume indicate a complete mastery of the material — gilded and polished bronze — which allows the light to circulate. Perfect surfaces and internal tension suggest an image of absoluteness and eternity, which is conducive to contemplation.

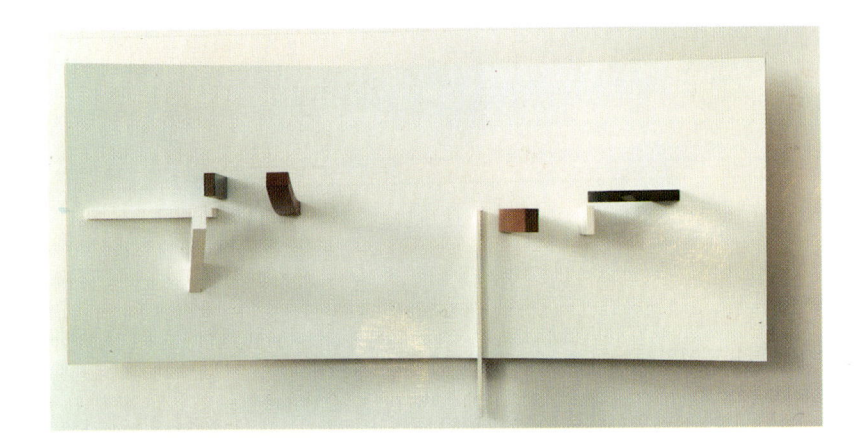

Victor Pasmore

Chelsham (Great Britain), 1908

Curved Relief Painting in White, Black and Indian Red

1962
Plywood covered with
synthetic resin, painted wood
61 x 121.7 x 21
Acquired with assistance from the
Fondation Abstraction et Carré, 1987

Victor Pasmore is, with Ben Nicholson, one of the most representative figures of British art to have used relief, as did a great number of European artists of his generation. The originality of the work shown here lies in the concave shape of the support and the highly protrusive elements, which project downwards, forwards, obliquely and sideways; either straight or curved, square or rectangular in section; painted white, black or Indian red. The arrangement of these shapes, their directions and the shadows they produce create a powerful, original rhythm.

P 907

1985
Acrylic on cardboard, mounted on canvas
100 x 300
Gift of the Fondation Abstraction
et Carré, 1987

Gottfried Honegger

Zurich (Switzerland), 1917

Gottfried Honegger has developed, on the fringes of Swiss Concrete Art and American abstraction, a most original body of work, where the links between determinism and chance are associated with an expression of sensibility towards the act of creation. This relief-painting is a good example of his approach. But if, in most of Honegger's work, chance was liable to interfere with the system which directed the execution, in *P 907* (P stands for Paris, where the work was produced), it plays no role. Here, the starting point is a square, the support being a multiple of it (basic square x 3), a dimension chosen with a view to the clear, legible development of the programme. The composition follows the increase in area of each element, from one eighth to one quarter of the area of the basic square, through a progressive increase in six phases of equal width, which give the six registers of the support. In the first phase, four rectangles, whose area is an eighth of that of the basic square are placed above each other (a cardboard surface mounted on the canvas and painted). In the last phase, there are two squares (each a quarter of the basic square in area), also made of cardboard mounted on the canvas. The intermediate phases leave a "remainder" at the top, painted white. These horizontal and vertical divisions create cadenzas; the smallest details of the support, the raised surface at the edges of the pieces of cardboard underlined by the light, and the contrast in texture between the mounted and the smooth surfaces — all these are elements of the pictorial language.

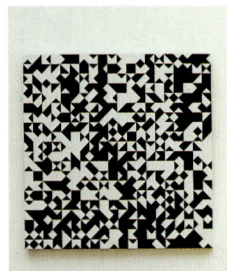

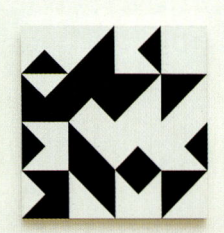

François Morellet

Cholet, 1926

Random Division of Triangles According to the Odd and Even Numbers in a Telephone Directory

1958
Oil on wood
80 x 80 for each of the three panels
Acquired in 1986

This remarkable triptych is the visual representation of its title: chance, in the guise of a series of numbers taken from a page of a telephone directory, dictates the distribution of triangles within a regular grid of squares. The image obtained by this system has no links with the sensibility of its author, and it was only on the completion of the first panel that he realized that he had created a dynamic, vibrant image through frequent repetitions of small, triangular forms, which contrast optically with the background. On a second panel of the same dimensions, the artist, in order to push forward even further the use of random effects, reproduced, in magnified form, a part of the first panel, i.e. the top left-hand square. Finally, the same approach was used for the third panel, with an enlarged triangle giving a large-scale reproduction of the top left-hand square of the second panel. Some Dadaist artists, such as Jean Arp and Sophie Taeuber-Arp, had used randomness previously, but it was with great rigour and elegance that François Morellet brought to a close the artistic reflection they had started, since any æsthetic judgment about his work also depends on our sensibility.

2,270 White Dots on a Lozenge

Pol Bury

Haine Saint Pierre (Belgium), 1922

1965
Wood, nylon, paint and electric motor
125 x 84
Acquired in 1983

This relief is comprised of a simple panel of waxed wood, to which is fixed a cluster of transparent nylon threads, each with a pearl-like drop of white paint at the tip. Moved by an electric motor, this assembly re-creates, through an almost imperceptible slowed-down motion and the very slight sound that accompanies it, manifestations of organic life which can only be noticed by concentrated attention, time and silence. Close to the Surrealist movement at the start of his career, Pol Bury never ceased to look for a poetic transformation of the most impoverished material, thus implying the denial of the act of artistic creation. He was using electric motors as early as 1957, and developed a body of work whose main theme was a slow, organic, underground movement, and whose forms were characterized by the strictest geometry, contrasting with the poverty of the materials. The work shown here is one of the most beautiful realizations of this theme, and it has given Bury a special place among the kinetic artists.

Pierre Soulages

Rodez, 1919

Painting, 28 November 1968

1968
Oil on canvas
220 x 365
Loaned by the artist, 1993

The size of this painting and the ratio between its height and its width are the primary elements of the formal language of the work. They divide up a space whose power and harmony cannot leave the viewer indifferent. The broad black marks that have invaded almost the whole of the canvas transform the white patches into light; they become a pulsation that creates the monumental quality of the work. Pierre Soulages tends to consider his paintings as plastic facts which give renewed sense to primitive perceptions; and he explains, in texts of great clarity, how his work resists literary forms of interpretation: "As the rhythm intensifies, an image — I mean the attempt to imbue it with a figurative association — becomes more and more impossible. If my painting does not touch any figurative anecdote, this is due, I believe, to the importance given to the rhythm, to the pulsation of forms in space, to the division of space by time." The means used by Soulages to express himself, with impulsion and restraint, profusion and penury, are a proof of his creative power.

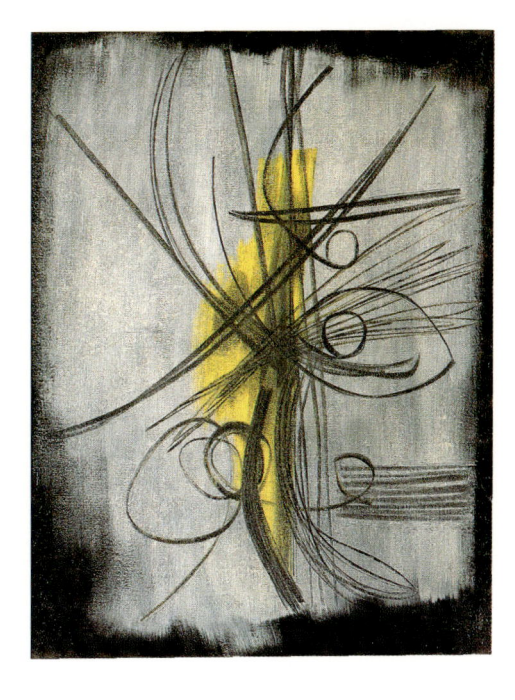

T 1949-22

1949
Oil on canvas
116.3 x 88.8
Gift of the artist, 1949

Hans Hartung

Leipzig (Germany), 1904
Antibes, 1989

As early as 1922, Hans Hartung considered that a splash could be a complete form of expression, and not simply a pretext for the construction of signifying forms. This can be seen in the present case, with splashes and graphic signs placed on a background where two colours — a light grey almost completely covering the black painted canvas— define a free space. A yellow splash spreads authoritatively in the vertical direction, and parallel horizontal strokes — a counterpoint — construct and give solidity to the space. On this foundation, a black calligraphic sign develops arabesques and striations, a trace in the air, an entirely mastered improvisation characteristic of Lyrical Abstraction, an artistic movement of which Hans Hartung is considered to be one of the main initiators.

Maria-Elena Vieira da Silva

Lisbon (Portugal), 1908
Paris, 1992

The Towers

1953
Oil on canvas
162 x 130
Acquired in 1956

Skyscrapers always fascinated Vieira da Silva, and one of the interesting aspects of this painting is the way the artist gives such edifices pictorial representation. The choice of colours — yellow, blue and white — suggests a night scene, seen from below in such a way as to present the wondrous aspect of steel and glass architecture, with its crystalline geometry. The composition is a grid of discontinuous vertical and horizontal lines, while a slight closing-in at the top produces an effect of perspective. Although inspired by direct observation of reality, the resulting image is an abstract re-creation influenced by the formal discipline of Cubism and the technique of the School of Paris.

The Cock, the Hen and the Chicken

1953
Marble
68 x 66.5 x 40.5
Acquired in 1988

Étienne Hadju

Turda (Rumania), 1907

Composed of three two-sided shapes of unequal size fixed to a plinth by hooks, this work redefines the art of sculpture in-the-round in a specific way: the elements are joined in the prolongation of their position to create a third dimension, while their flat, smooth aspect relates them to bas-relief. At the beginning of his career, Hadju declared: "I always wanted to enter the volume [...] I wondered how a volume could be expressed through the plane." Cycladic art helped him to realize this aspiration; as can be seen in the sculpture shown here, he used similar abstracted, slightly allusive forms to put across the signification: in this case, the indentations of the cockscomb, the pointed beak of the hen, the roundness of the chicken. The art of his sculpture leads the light onto the surface in such a way as to reveal the details of the volume; the marble used by Hadju is so thin that the outlines are seen with great sharpness and precision. To these characteristics, which he found in Cycladic statuary, Hadju finally adds a technique that reveals the volume at points where the marble is so thin that it is permeable to light, and indeed is penetrated by it.

Nicolas de Staël

Saint Petersburg (Russia), 1914
Antibes, 1955

Sicily

1954
Oil on canvas
114 x 146
Acquired in 1982

Painted near the end of his life, this landscape is a magnificent example of de Staël's return to figuration and to the genres which traditionally codified it. Here, a new technique was invented: the pictorial plane, which he had previously organized in rectangles, was extended into broad, luminous areas of bright colours, applied with the palette knife, and through it the canvas can at times be seen. The lower half of the painting draws the eye towards a red square in the centre, through a simple architectural structure of triangular planes which suggests a distant perspective. The dissonance of the violet in the middle of the expanse of yellow, which is also seen in the green of the sky, and the vibration where green and red meet — all this expresses the blinding sunlight. This last period of the School of Paris' most famous painter brought to an end a career in which formal experimentation had always been linked to experimentation with paint.

Blue at Evening in Royan

Olivier Debré

1965
Oil on canvas
189 x 194
Acquired in 1968

Paris, 1920

This painting, whose title refers to the time and place which inspired it, is characteristic of the manner Olivier Debré invented in 1963. The broad expanse of the canvas is covered with a large area of blue pigment spread out in a fluid fashion: three irregular gaps, at the edges of the canvas, cut through the blue surface, producing the illusion of a third dimension. Olivier Debré is one of the main exponents of the abstract landscape movement, whose main features are colour lyricism and gesturality; *Blue at Evening in Royan* thus stands half-way between figurative and abstract art.

Jean Dubuffet

Le Havre, 1901
Paris, 1985

Mire G 137 (Kowloon)

1983
Acrylic on paper, mounted on canvas
134 x 200
Acquired in 1985

This work belongs to the series "Les Mires" (exhibited at the 1984 Venice Biennial) and features an apparently spontaneous, rapidly executed graphism. The final work is made up of four surfaces of identical dimensions brought together — edge to edge and without a frame — in line with the suggestion of a concept worked out beforehand: one can imagine an infinite series of identical rectangles where an equal density of lines and a precise distribution of colour is given by compulsive repetition. In 1942, Dubuffet rejected what he thought to be the conventions of painting and the traditional concept of beauty. Confronted with a culture he believed to be moribund, he tried to reach the zero degree of art, where expression would be rooted in mental activity. From his last works, such as the Grenoble series, it is obvious that he never wavered in his belief that the task of art was to make manifest the primitive values of the mind. The subtitle of the work, *Kowloon* (an Asian town), reminds us that Dubuffet was engaged in literary activity, concurrently with his career as a painter.

Night's Collar

1985
Plaster, passementerie and diverse materials
220 x 165 x 70
Acquired in 1993-1994

Étienne-Martin

Loriol, 1913

Night's Collar belongs to the "Demeures" cycle, which the artist began in 1954. The materials and the shape of the work are reminiscent of the 1962 *Manteau (Demeure 5)*, now in the Musée National d'Art Moderne, in Paris, and turn it into a kind of protective clothing, blanket, second skin — house, mother, suit of armour. With its various materials (plaster, carpet, ropes, wire-netting, mirrors, paint, etc.) and their colours, the work stands midway between a ceremonial dress and a totem. The way it is situated in space defines the work as an all-round sculpture, whose interpretation is a complex task made even more difficult by the enigmatic, magical character of its composition.

Tom Wesselman

Cincinnati, Ohio, 1931

Bedroom Painting N° 31

1973
Oil on canvas
207 x 262
Acquired in 1974

In this painting, which shows a naked, supine woman and a bunch of flowers, reference is made to the huge printed or painted billboards that are to be found in urban areas. In the sixties, Wesselman was already working on the nude in series of works inspired by Matisse and by posters. With his models, superimposed like filters on reality, Wesselman questions the reciprocal relations of art, reality and advertising. As an eternal archetype of beauty, the naked female body is also a stereotype elaborated with the lens of a camera, flattened by a close-up which places all the objects depicted in the space of the canvas. The monumental format is that of advertising posters, and the technique juxtaposes different styles: volumes, flat areas, *trompe-l'œil* of printed photographic images, and painting. The image created by Wesselman presents reality as the sum of numerous tricks.

Life is so Complex

1966
Perspex mounted on wood
12 elements, each 50 x 65
Acquired in 1968

Martial Raysse

Golfe Juan, 1936

This puzzle-portrait is made up of twelve elements, four of which are repeated twice: some parts of the face are missing, others are repeated but shown differently. Painted with aerosols on Perspex, the work is an answer to the desire to "use modern techniques to express a modern world." New Realism, of which Martial Raysse is one of the main exponents in France, has shown that this world consists of social clichés. Thus, the face of the woman is coded, and can be recognized through signs such as eyes made up in black, mouth painted red, smooth complexion, cheek perfectly curved. The title of the work is a cliché in English, and shows the American hold on popular culture generated by a society which Martial Raysse imagines as "new, sterilized and pure, and also at one with the techniques used, with technological discoveries."

Jacques Monory

Paris, 1934

Murder N° 2

1968
Oil on canvas
229 x 196
Acquired in 1978

During the sixties, Jacques Monory was one of the main exponents in France of Narrative Figuration, a current within New Figuration. *Murder N° 2* belongs to a series of twenty-five autobiographical paintings. The scene shown here is divided into two parts — images of a murder shown live, and the murder of the artist, whose identity is concealed by having his eyes covered with a black rectangle. Jacques Monory uses the specific vocabulary of photography and the cinema (framing, viewing angles, etc.), which gives the composition a certain rigour. Movement, which in films increases the feeling of reality, is expressed in painting by a series of stroboscopic images. The strict composition, the monochrome colour and the smooth technique give the scene an anonymous quality external to present time, where reality and fiction are apparently brought together.

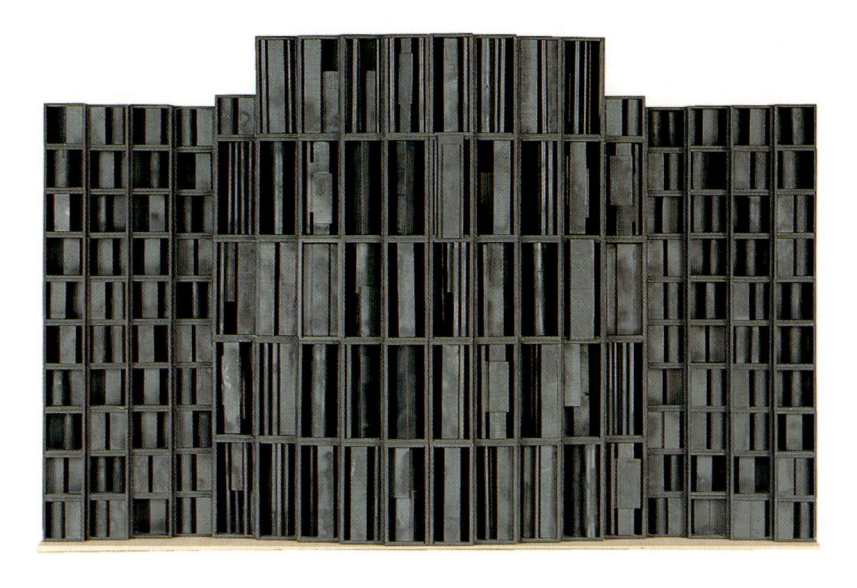

Shadow and Reflection

1966
Painted wood
273 x 430 x 65
Acquired in 1969

Louise Nevelson

Kiev (Ukraine), 1900
New York, N. Y., 1988

It was in 1957 that Louise Nevelson began creating boxes, which she occasionally put together to form wall reliefs. The Museum of Grenoble's relief resembles a triptych with a convex central part made up of rectangular boxes, while those of the two lateral wings — concave and smaller — are square. This modular, very geometric composition, where vertical and horizontal lines are in equilibrium, is also a contrast and interplay of shadows and reflections, hollow and raised parts, flat and curved surfaces, formed by the repetitive elements inside the boxes. The black colour, which is spread over the whole structure, heightens the mystery of the shadows. The art of assemblage, initiated by Cubism and often used by the Dadaists, is certainly the main influence behind *Shadow and Reflection*, but Louise Nevelson brought renewed experimentation to these movements during her stay in Mexico, from 1949 to 1951. Her sombre work is certainly related to Mexico's highly baroque and often tormented forms of religious art.

Sam Francis

San Mateo, California, 1923

From a Coral Cauldron

1969
Acrylic on canvas
200 x 351
Acquired in 1976

When explaining the work he did in the sixties, Sam Francis says he considers "the broad central area [of his paintings] not as an empty space, but as a monumental shape, defined by narrow, shredded colour strips at the edges." This painting appears to be both hedonistic and constructivist: after setting very controlled limits, he uses a very fluid pigment whose brightness is increased by transparence. There are no possibilities for correction, and splashes are made use of with great pleasure. Thus, Sam Francis' paint covers and sculpts a space he has previously defined by masking. This technique is reminiscent of the gestural painting of Monet when he painted the *Nymphéas* as an "environment painting", and, of course, Jackson Pollock's action painting. Sam Francis is indebted to these two painters for the importance attributed to colour, and the creation of a free, open space revealed by colour.

Anitou N° 3

1958
Oil on canvas
Diam. 144
Acquired in 1992

Leon Polk Smith

Chickasha, Oklahoma, 1906

Leon Polk Smith played a major role in the evolution of American painting after 1945: he was the precursor of Hard Edge, a reaction against Abstract Expressionism within New Abstraction. He analyzed Mondrian's work, and his thinking, based on the interchangeability of form with the space of the pictorial field, led him to the use of curved lines. His concepts were presented in a series of circular paintings, the *Tondi*, to which *Anitou N° 3* belongs. He uses a free line which echoes the format of the painting and divides the surface into two opposed zones that are also linked like pieces of a jigsaw puzzle. The colour, applied in a neutral way, and the precise, rigorous outlines, give perfect flatness to the surface. In this curved space, the artist plays with the ambiguous, conflicting relations between form and content, positive and negative — this is made possible by his reduced palette: an extreme contrast of black and white vibrating with great intensity.

Brice Marden

Bronxville, N. Y., 1938

Join

1973
Oil paint and wax on canvas
184 x 305 (76.5 + 76.5 + 152)
Acquired in 1973

This painting is made up of three rectangular panels placed side by side and painted in different tones of coloured grey. The symmetry of the composition (the width of the large panel is the sum of the widths of the other two) is disrupted by the organization of the colours: the components of the painting — form, colour and surface — are balanced in an interactive relationship that instigates the harmony of the work. Each monochrome panel was painted in successive layers until it attained the appearance of a uniform, smooth screen; the wax added to the pigments gives strength to these screens, and increases the fullness of the colour, which appears as a compact block of the same dimensions as the support. A dense, mysterious light radiates out from the painting: "To my mind," declared Brice Marden, "the emotional intensity of these paintings should preclude any kind of intellectual or technical approach; they have to be felt, that's all."

Robert Mangold

Distorted Square Within a Square

North Tonawanda, N. Y., 1937

1974
Acrylic and white pencil on canvas
167.6 x 167.6
Acquired in 1991

The perfectly square format of this monochrome painting shows only a line drawn with a white pencil: a distorted square touching the edges of the canvas at three corners. It provides a summary of what is, according to Mangold, the essence of painting: shape, surface, colour and line. Shape, and primarily the square, is for him the only "perfectly rigorous [shape] evoking nothing." The uniform colour is sprayed with an airbrush, and is made up of an undetermined mixture of ochres. The irregularity of the inscribed square wrong-foots the viewer's perception and disrupts the balance of the painting. Close to Minimal Art, from which he borrows the space-plan, the frontal view, the elementariness and the unity, Mangold introduces into the seemingly obvious aspect of his work subtle dissonances of colour and line. With this kind of ambiguity, which is reminiscent of Mannerism, painting can be re-invented.

Sol LeWitt

Hartford, Connecticut, 1928

White Five-Part Modular Piece

1971
Painted steel
157 x 725 x 236
Acquired in 1973

With this sculpture, Sol LeWitt was looking for an elementary form with which he could create a work devoid of anecdote, referring only to its own operative mode. The basic module is a cube reduced to its sides; built up out of steel bars of square sections, painted white — an inexpressive colour, according to LeWitt — this module is repeated five times, in two staggered rows, directly on the floor. Being machine-made, its precision is completely impersonal. In such a work, the idea is that of "a machine producing art", an art defined as conceptual, but whose realization is essential since, if it is true that the quantity, format, environment and colour of elements are subjective and appear to be external to the logic of this art, they are nevertheless a function of the definition given to sculpture by its history (thus format, depending on whether the work is destined for an interior or an exterior, enables sculpture to be distinguished from architectural and other objects). The transparence of the Grenoble work gives a simultaneous vision of the inside space, whose limits are the edges of the cubes, and of the outside space, the setting of the installation. The succession of cubes invites the viewer to walk around them, and grasp the work in its totality, as well as its interaction with its environment.

Flander Field

1978
Red cedar
90 x 30 x 30
(dimensions of each of the 54 elements)
Presented by the FNAC (Fonds National
d'Art Contemporain) in 1987

Carl Andre

Quincy, Massachusetts, 1935

A leading figure of Minimal Art, Carl Andre has elaborated a formal vocabulary based on three fundamental notions: the use of raw materials, modular compositions, the flatness of the sculptural work considered as a site.
In *Flander Field*, the artist has placed 54 elements directly on the ground: beams cut by machine, of identical dimensions and without the slightest trace of work done by hand. Each element shows its imperfections right away, and it is in this materiality that a meaning must be sought. The work has no plinth, and is on the same scale as the viewer, so that the immediacy of perception is increased. The beams, separated by regular intervals, are placed in rows so as to form a rectangle on the ground. This distribution, with no hierarchical organization of the elements, gives emphasis to the horizontal dimension: the whole set of standing beams is seen as a single surface. The elements are separated by a void, and appear as autonomous entities, juxtaposed without being assembled, and brought together by nothing more than the pre-established order decided on by the artist. Carl Andre thus rejects the notion of composition, and transforms his sculpture into a site. "I conceive of sculpture as a road. A road isn't revealed to us at any of its points, no privileged viewpoint exists for seeing it [...], we have to travel, drive on the road, or walk by the side of it..."

Donald Judd

Yellow Wallpiece

Excelsior Springs, Missouri, 1928
New York, N. Y., 1994

1987
Wood, plywood and Perspex
100 x 100 x 50 for each box
Presented by the FNAC (Fonds National
d'Art Contemporain) in 1990

With his interest in the elaboration of a "Minimal" art — immediately perceived by the viewer — Donald Judd uses relief because, according to him, in this type of expression, "what counts is the integrity of the piece, its immediate perception." Thus, *Yellow Wallpiece* is made up of four identical square boxes; separated by regular intervals and aligned two by two — vertically and horizontally — they form a square on the wall, and the space between them is in the shape of a cross. The inside space of the boxes is divided by vertical planks — either perpendicular to or at an angle with the back. As a locus of contrast between the visible and the invisible, between shadow and light, between strongly coloured area and raw material, the boxes are sensitive to the modulation of the light. Since there is no traditional structure and no hierarchical organization, the independence of each volume is all the greater; as isolated elements they assert their quality of "specific objects"; it is only through the mathematical progression which directs their internal divisions that they can be seen as parts, integrated into a homogeneous whole.

Fig. 135 — La droite D' représente la fonction $y = 2x + 1$.

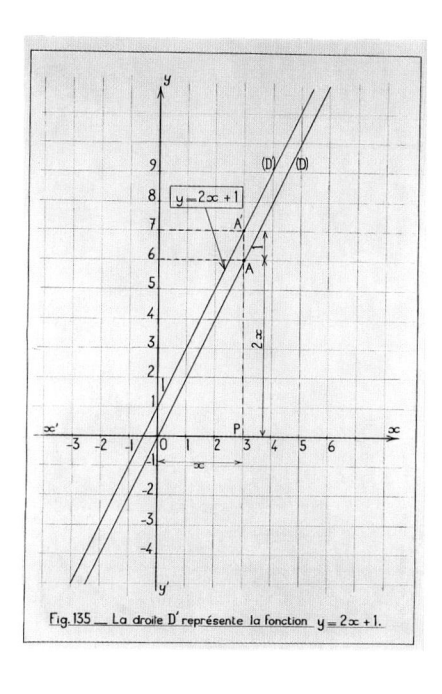

The Straight Line D' Represents the Function Y = 2x + 1

1966
Acrylic on canvas
168 x 116
Acquired in 1987

Bernar Venet

Saint Auban, 1941

As the first French exponent of Conceptual Art, which was revealed by two exhibitions in 1969, Bernar Venet was able to find a specific position within this movement of contemporary art whose most radical expressions occurred in Anglo-Saxon countries. In this painting the artist transferred onto canvas — by hand and on a larger scale — the graphic representation of the function given in the title. The choice of a subject taken from the rational field of mathematics excludes any possibility of generating different readings by reducing the painting to a single interpretation. The artist only intervenes in the choice of subject, the realization being more or less automatic. Thus defying the values normally attached to the act of creation, Bernar Venet limits his work to copying, and restricts the artist's virtuosity to the faithful reproduction of data. Bernar Venet's approach is radical, and he pushes back the limits of the work's existence — the viewer is not offered other interpretational levels, and the work only reflects the evidence of its presence. Paradoxically, when removed from its original domain, the mathematical function used by Bernar Venet can be seen and understood as a work of art, and thus loses its original objectivity and neutrality.

Claude Viallat

Nîmes, 1936

Untitled

1972
Oil on canvas
266 x 197
Acquired in 1974

Viallat's painting is the repetition, on an unstretched canvas, of the same shape that he has been using since 1966: the print left by a simple daub of the kind of sponge that is used to whitewash walls in the South of France, where Viallat comes from. The materialist analysis that Claude Viallat was to undertake in the Support-Surface group, when he tried to move painting out of its traditional framework by deconstructing it, is enriched by an almost ritual practice of repetition in the gesture of the painter.

Marks left by a N° 50 Brush Repeated at Regular Intervals of 30 cm

1986
Acrylic on polycanvas
330 x 214
Acquired in 1988

Niele Toroni

Locarno-Muralto (Switzerland), 1937

The "work/painting" method used by Toroni in all his work is revealed by the title. It remains the same whether Toroni paints a support, with or without stretcher, or, as is most often the case, in close links with an architectural space. The basic structure of his activity is a series of brushstrokes in staggered rows. This structure is ceaselessly repeated, to the exclusion of any expression, pictorial value, form, composition or symbolism. For Toroni, it has value as work: he is the person who is painting, and his work should be seen since its spatial disposition produces infinite variations. Among the artists of the B.M.P.T. group (as it was named by the critics — Daniel Buren, Olivier Mosset, Michel Parmentier, Niele Toroni), Toroni is the only one who never changed his stance. Like Diogenes, with his contempt for honours, riches and social conventions, he pursues his work with an intellectual rigour that makes him reject anything superfluous. Since the death of painting, so often announced by the avant-gardes of our century, he can be taken as the model of the painter.

Michel Parmentier

Paris, 1938

Untitled

1967
Oil on canvas
247 x 229
Acquired in 1977

This work was produced according to the process used by the artist for all his output: the systematic repetition of horizontal bands, 38 cm wide, whose colour (which changes each year) alternates with the bare surface; the paint is sprayed on, the bare part of the support being protected by folding the canvas. From the act of painting, Parmentier retains only the zero degree of representation, the image of the paint as materiality itself. He announced, "I paint paint", and can be said to share, with the member of the B.M.P.T. group (Daniel Buren, Olivier Mosset, Michel Parmentier, Niele Toroni), the belief that "art is a distraction, art is false." His sixteen years of inactivity, between 1968 and 1983, were the extension of his subversive activities, which have been considered to be close to that of the other members of the B.M.P.T. group.

Blooded

1983
Photographic prints under glass
302 x 252
Acquired in 1987

Gilbert and George

Dolomites (Italy), 1943 [Gilbert]
Devon (Great Britain), 1942 [George]

Blooded consists of twenty-five photographic prints forming a monumental work. The black edges of the prints and the simplified shapes, as well as the broad areas of flat colour, are reminiscent of the art of stained glass. This reference is brought out even more clearly by the fact that *Blooded* is a parody of religious images: Gilbert and George are shown sitting back to back, leaning against a dead tree trunk; they are singing their love for the world; a flower blooms in front of each of them, while blood flowing from above evokes the destruction of the natural world. The work of George and Gilbert, which is essentially polemical, produces an image that is shocking in its very simplification and humour.

Jannis Kounellis

Piræus (Greece), 1936

Untitled

1985
Hessian sacks and paint
320 x 60 (height varies according to the wall)
Acquired in 1989

Hessian sacks, folded in four and stacked in a regular order, form a parallelepiped against a wall painted black from floor to ceiling, and whose width is equal to that of the pile of sacks, which still smell strongly of hessian and of the grain they contained. The matt, intense black colour suggests combustion as well as the void. With this extremely simple assemblage, Kounellis transposes various relations and contrasts: volume and plane, matter and paint, reality and abstraction, organic and manufactured products, the experienced and the symbolic. Those rough and ready materials are set up without any technical knowledge in a composition that requires constant adaptation, though in fact all one needs to know of it is what the artist's intentions were — this is a new definition of art. Kounellis, an exponent of Arte Povera, ends up creating an image whose power of evocation derives from the materials as well as from the will that brought them together.

Rebel Moon

Rebecca Horn

1991
Ten typewriters fixed on a metal bar,
a glass cone containing mercury
Variable length (depending on the site),
height approx. 3.50 m
Acquired in 1992

Michelstadt (Germany), 1944

Rebecca Horn's complex approach, though impossible to classify, stands out clearly in this work made up of found objects which have been diverted from their original function and are presented in a paradoxical fashion. Ten typewriters are suspended from a beam just under the ceiling, keyboards pointing towards the floor. The keys of each machine are struck by an electrically-operated striker to produce a clicking noise, and the tinkle of the carriage returns can also be heard. The whole work, which is of great enigmatic intensity, evokes the hammering of birds' beaks in the forest. At one extremity, two of the typewriters are so close that electric sparks dart between them as a sign of their amorous relationship. On the floor is a glass cone filled with mercury, whose shape, together with its shadow on the ground, increases the symbolic power of the whole. This work, with its varied elements, the sounds it produces — abstract as well as natural — and its disturbing presentation in space, has a strong poetic dimension that gives an indication of the artist's pantheist vision.

Tony Cragg

Liverpool (Great Britain), 1949

Three Shelves, Wine Bottles

1981
3 shelves, wine bottles
350 x 450
Acquired in 1988

Tony Cragg is the leading artist of the new British sculpture which sprang up at the end of the seventies; he mainly uses found material, either unchanged or with a slight transformation. *Three Shelves, Wine Bottles* shows his interest in the urban, industrial world. Cragg likes objects for their plastic, symbolic qualities — here he concentrates on the image of the bottle, which he multiplies. This multiplication process leads to an ordered composition contrasting with the imbalance, on the wall, of the three shelves on which the bottles are fixed. The general lines suggest a dynamic movement close to that of the Suprematists: the empty bottles, which are waste products as much as they are pure volumes, give emphasis, through their arrangement, to the precariousness of the world. Through its integration into this original composition, the object is given a new interpretation, and its image transformed.

Perfect Vehicles

1988
Plaster, paint, acrylic, 30 vases
(22 x 22 x 50) on bases of various heights
Installation: 500 x 700 x 168
Acquired in 1989

Allan McCollum

Los Angeles, California, 1944

McCollum's objects strongly resemble industrial artefacts: they are produced in large numbers; within any given series the variations are minute, as though to make comparison possible; the finish is perfect, the colours usually attractive; the presentation system emphasizes multiplicity, and thereby the possibility of choice; and finally, the material used is cheap and ordinary. McCollum chose, between 1979 and 1984, a shape reminiscent of decorative Chinese vases, so widespread as to be absolutely neutral. One cannot be sure whether these mock-ups are a parody of everyday objects or of works of art. The vases, which have been mass-produced, could be thought of as commercial objects, and their presentation would tend to suggest this; the installation and its staging, as conceived by the artist, are those of a department store. However, the colour and base of each vase is unique, as well as obviously useless and false — and this is meant to elevate the whole to the stature of a work of art. As it is, this installation, which is of such neutrality that it tends to irritate, enables viewers to exercise their own critical judgement.

Helmut Federle

Soleure (Switzerland), 1944

McArthur Park

1987
Acrylic on canvas
220 x 330
Presented by the FNAC (Fonds National d'Art Contemporain) in 1989

Strongly influenced by American painting, especially that of Barnett Newman and Clyfford Still, the abstract work of Helmut Federle is highly charged, in all its austerity, with a spiritual content: form, colour and composition should, according to him, be a quest for the essential, and express the anguish of being confronted with the void and with death. The composition is organized along broad horizontal and vertical lines; where they cross, they suggest the artist's initials, in the bold letters of a headline. Within a rectangular format, close to a square, a powerful, balanced structure of grey lines stands out against a chromatically undefined, paler background. The oscillation of the background colour from green to a dirty yellow, the rough texture, the matt aspect, the contrast between light and dark tones — all this shows clearly that the real subject of the painting is the interplay between shadow and light.

Annette Messager

Berck, 1943

My Greetings

1989
Black and white photographs under glass
300 x 100
Acquired in 1992

The subject of My Greetings is a photographic representation of the human body; it is presented as an accumulation of body fragments. The elements under glass make up a dense, saturated relief, full of contrasts: between the black and white of the photographs, and between the simple, flat surface they create — here a triangle — and the tangle of strings holding them. The body fragments are framed in such a way, and with such strong chiaroscuro, that they become altered representations of nature. These images, rendered abnormal by their tight juxtaposition and superposition, are the opposite of what the camera lens was meant to fix: a subjective vision, produced by caprice and emotion, half-way between fantasy and chimera. This vision concatenates the single and the multiple, and contaminates the forms. The optical riddle thus created is a supreme exercise of freedom.

Christian Boltanski

Monument

Paris, 1944

1985
Photographs, light bulbs and electric wire
3.50 x 10 m
Acquired in 1985

Given the size and symmetrical arrangement of this work — whose three "panels" are shaped like the a triptych in a church — it can definitely be termed a monument. The light of the electric bulbs which form the outline of the work increase this effect by forcing the viewer to remain at the distance necessary to all the mechanisms meant for commemoration.

Indeed, the purpose here is to evoke the memory of the children whose faces are presented by framed black and white photographs surrounded by a halo of light. Only later does one realize that the installation is a makeshift job: the electric wires are too long, and trail all over the place, the photographs are grey, framed with paper used for wrapping presents. Boltanski's setup maintains a balance between the serious — the tragic, even — and the absurd. His work organizes on the wall, in a minimal order rooted in the history of forms and ritual ceremonies, life fragments magnified by the light. This is how he returns to the art of the *Vanitas*, where the surroundings — representing richness and duration — are placed side by side with elements representing the triumph of death. In this work, photography is a *trompe-l'œil*; it presents us with little more than the illusion of life, and contributes a dramatic dimension to the *Vanitas*. It is thus that, in Boltanski's work, a profound reflection on the means of creation — a combination of the most contemporary with the most traditional — can be recognized.

Bertrand Lavier

Châtillon sur Seine, 1949

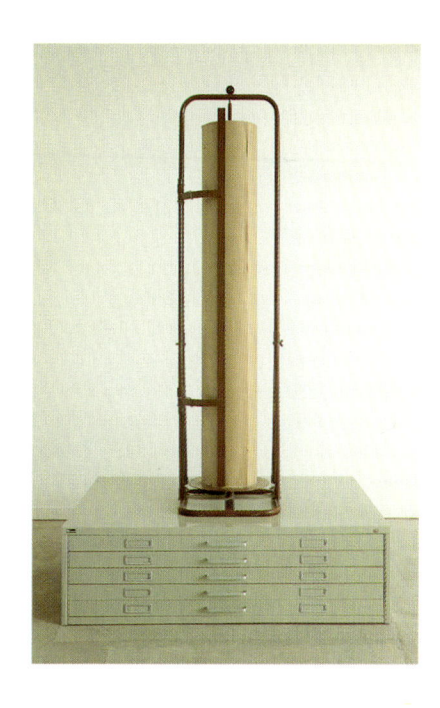

Manutan / Kind

1987
Kraft paper dispenser
on drawing cabinet
227 x 135 x 95
Acquired in 1988

With Manutan/Kind Bertrand Lavier created a sculpture by placing a Kraft paper dispenser on a drawing cabinet, the title of the work being simply the names of the manufacturers of the two objects, which retain their own identity, and together form a sculpture on a plinth. The combination is governed by formal motivations. The incongruity and formal quality of this assemblage create a dynamism through which the coupling can be identified as a new form, while, in an analytical vision, one can apprehend the drawing cabinet which, by its shape, evokes a plinth on which is placed, like a sculpture in itself, the dispenser. Thus, from the everyday reality of manufactured objects, Lavier — with all the seriousness of his reflection — abolishes the frontiers between life and art, between the real and its representation.

Drawings Collection 203

Tour de l'Isle

ANCIENT DRAWINGS

Italian Drawings

The museum's collection of ancient drawings, with almost 5,000 works, consists essentially of a bequest made in 1890 by Léonce Mesnard, who was an enlightened amateur — the collection of paintings, objets d'art and drawings he had acquired was the finest in Grenoble. This highly varied collection was particularly rich in works from the Italian School, with a large number of drawings by recognized masters. The 830 items are presently being studied, and specialists have agreed that most of the attributions made by Mesnard were correct; when changes had to be made, it was often to raise the value of a work.

There are some drawings from the 15th century, one of the most interesting of which, the *Saint Jerome* from Lombardy, was found recently among the German drawings. It is a rare piece, full of the intense, precise poetry found in late 15th century northern Italian works.

The 16th century collection is fairly complete, with, besides the Venetians (who will be discussed below), a large number of Florentine Mannerist drawings (Salviatti, Poccetti), as well as drawings from Genoa (Cambiaso) and Rome (Zuccaro).

Among the Mannerists, Parmigianino's *Woman with Outstretched Arms* is a fine example of this artist's virtuosity and elegance. The undulating lines and the slender hands and feet emphasize the restlessness produced by the rapidity of the draftsmanship.

Most of the artistic centres of the Italian Seicento are also represented, from Milan to Naples, and especially some towering Baroque figures: Pietro da Cortona and Giovanni Battista Gaulli, also known as Baciccio, whose *Two Warriors Fighting* radiates an ardour that shows him to have been a great decorator. The assurance of the pen line and the sharp contrasts make the figures in this preliminary sketch appear to spring out from the surface of the paper.

Lombard School

15th century

Saint Jerome in the Desert

Pen and brown ink, brown wash,
white gouache highlights on beige paper
15.5 x 11.8
Léonce Mesnard bequest, 1890

Parmigianino

(Francesco Mazzola)

Parma (Italy), 1503
Casal Maggiore (Italy), 1540

Woman with Outstretched Arms

Black chalk, pen and black ink,
grey wash on blue paper
15.3 x 12.5
Léonce Mesnard bequest, 1890

Baciccio

(Giovanni Batista Gaulli)

Genoa (Italy), 1639
Rome (Italy), 1709

Two Warriors Fighting

Pen and black ink, grey wash
on beige paper
28.5 x 39.6
Léonce Mesnard bequest, 1890

Venice

Some of the great Venetian painters are known to have been tireless draughtsmen who produced large quantities of studies which were often as magnificent as their paintings, and at times more highly appreciated. This was the case for Jacopo Palma Giovane, whose works in oil, which were overshadowed by the giant masters of the 16th century, especially Tintoretto, are probably less representative of his work than his numerous, extremely brilliant drawings.

The study shown here belongs to a series of drawings which Léonce Mesnard bought in one of the important auctions where he was an assiduous bidder. The technique, pen and wash, was Palma's favourite, and he used it without preparation, frenetically, in his pursuit of the perfect line.

One of this series of drawings was recently attributed to Veronese, namely the impressive *Page of Studies*; both sides of the paper have been drawn on, with an incredible number of figures that were to be used for a stage set. This is a typical example of what was intended to be a means of pinning down the runaway imagination of the artist, and such sketches, though originally treated as mere first drafts, are nowadays venerated as masterpieces in their own right.

After the traditional lacuna of the 17th century, the Venetians make a comeback with some very beautiful sketches by Diziani and, of course, Giambattista and Giandomenico Tiepolo. Those of the latter's works which are owned by the museum include a very beautiful *Study of Animals*. Rather than reproduce yet another example, however beautiful, of Giambattista's celebrated work in pen and brown wash, we have decided to show a page of sketches: this is a recent — and fascinating — attribution, showing the classical side, soft and imposing, of an artist who has often been a victim of critical oversimplification.

Jacopo Palma Giovane

Venice (Italy), 1544-1628

Studies of Mythological Figures

Pen and brown ink,
brown wash on cream-coloured paper
21 x 22.1
Léonce Mesnard bequest, 1890

Veronese

(Paolo Caliari)

Verona (Italy), 1528
Venice (Italy), 1588

Page of Studies

Pen and brown ink,
brown wash on cream paper
26.6 x 18.3
Léonce Mesnard bequest, 1890

Giambattista Tiepolo

Venice (Italy), 1696
Madrid (Spain), 1770

Study of Hands and Draperies

Red chalk on beige paper
24.3 x 36.8
Léonce Mesnard bequest, 1890

Drawings from the Northern Schools

All the Northern schools are represented in the collection. Among the German drawings, which number about 90, there are works of great quality. Some very important artists are present in the Flemish collection, and a real masterpiece was found among Jordaens' drawings. It is a large allegorical composition whose subject is explained in a cartouche: Truth is shown, masked, to the prince, and only time will reveal her identity. The drawing is characteristic of the composite technique often used by Jordaens, who, not only mixed gouache, watercolours and chalks of various shades, but would also stick together a number of sheets of paper, as if his incomparable Baroque verve had difficulty in finding a material support on which to express itself.

In the Dutch collection, which is our most complete, the drawing by Rembrandt masks the talent of many minor painters, but a number of series by important artists give a sound structure to the collection.

Among the landscape painters, next to Poelenburgh and van Goyen, who are represented by a single beautiful piece each, the museum owns sets by, for example, Molijn and Breenbergh. Breenbergh's *Roman Ruins* are a perfect example of a central tendency of the first half of the 17th century, when landscapes filled with antique ruins started to define one of the settings of the classical period that was to follow. In Breenbergh's drawings, the soft contrasts rendered in a light wash, express a serenity that is in perfect agreement with the subject. Also shown here is a highly original study attributed to another artist whose work is well represented in the collection: Herman Van Saftleven. His *Rock by the Water* is an astonishing, masterful translation of the way nature was apprehended in 17th century Holland.

Bartholomeus Breenbergh

Deventer (Netherlands), c. 1599-1600
Amsterdam (Netherlands), before 1657

Roman Ruins

c. 1629
Black chalk, brown wash on cream paper
15 x 21.2
Léonce Mesnard bequest, 1890

Herman Van Saftleven

Rotterdam (Netherlands), 1609
Utrecht (Netherlands), 1685

Rock by the Water

Black chalk on cream paper
20.1 x 29.6
Léonce Mesnard bequest, 1890

Jacob Jordaens

Antwerp (Antwerp), 1593-1678

The Prince, Truth and Time

Black chalk, red chalk,
watercolour and gouache on beige paper
50.6 x 40.2
Acquired in 1858

The French 17th Century

As in most of the other collections of drawings held by French museums, the "grand siècle", so important in the history of French art, is well represented in Grenoble. There are about 130 drawings from this period, starting with an anonymous *Rape of the Sabine Women* dating from the second half of the 16th century, and which is a beautiful example of French Mannerism. The main tendencies of the period and the great qualities of the artists, from archaism to the pictorial style of La Fosse, are shown.

The *Crucifixion* by Jean Boucher de Bourges, who is now recognized as one of the most influential artists of the first third of the 17th century, clearly shows his contribution to French Classicism. His knowledge of the Italians and the ancient masters gives his drawings a serene plenitude that ensured the success of his career. Another dazzling career, acted out in Paris, was that of Vouet, who, to simplify matters, is thought as the importer of Italian Baroque into France. His famous studies of single figures, done mostly for stage sets, are nevertheless imbued with a majesty that reminds us that some of the greatest classical painters were his students. His *Man Fleeing*, which has no links with any of his paintings, has the rapidity of the drawings of the 1630s.

We then come to some beautiful, purely classical drawings, such as the work of Charles Mellin (often confused, as far as his drawings are concerned, with Poussin) and the large *Apotheosis of Hercules* by Le Brun; to represent the end of the century, there is Louis de Boullogne's *Apollo and Daphne*, an illustration full of vitality. One of the characteristics of this golden age of French drawing was brilliant technique, which is why preliminary studies, with their virtuoso white highlights, were much sought after by collectors. The subject of this drawing, taken from Ovid's *Metamorphoses*, is one of the most evocative in the poetic repertoire of the reign of the Sun King.

Boucher de Bourges

(Jean Boucher)

Bourges, 1568-1633

Crucifixion

Black chalk on beige paper
29.1 x 19.2
Source unknown

Simon Vouet

Paris, 1590-1640

Man Fleeing

Black chalk, white chalk highlights
on beige paper
34.8 x 24.2
Léonce Mesnard bequest, 1890

Louis de Boullogne the Younger

Paris, 1654-1733

Apollo and Daphne

Black chalk, grey wash, white gouache
highlights on brown paper
Léonce Mesnard bequest, 1890

The French 18th Century

Containing over 500 drawings, this section of the collection is one of its most fascinating subjects for study. The extraordinary number of 18th century French artists and the variety of genres they practised explain why their drawings are so interesting. The Grenoble collection, ranging from unknown landscape artists to drawings by Fragonard, is a mirror of the eclecticism of its donor, Léonce Mesnard.

The century opens with a small sketch of extraordinary verve, once thought to be by Gillot, but now reattributed to Watteau. It contrasts with the period that immediately preceded it, and looks forward to a period of pure virtuosity — the triumph of Boucher, Natoire and Fragonard, of whose work the museum holds several magnificent examples, from landscapes to religious compositions, such as the two studies, in black chalk and wash, of the *Dream of Saint Joseph*.

The most spectacular works are those of the second half of the century. Doyen's *Martyrdom of Saint Sebastian*, a theatrical drawing, almost Wagnerian before its time, stands in opposition to Neoclassicism and leads directly to the most impetuous works of the 19th century. The white gouache, brutally applied, could even be said to have something in common with Expressionist lighting.

The same technique, but used in a totally different spirit, led to the *Frieze in the Antique Style* by David, which he drew after returning from his first stay in Rome, in 1780. The repertoire and composition are pure Classicism, though the three Fates on the right are reminiscent of Boucher, a painter whom David had always admired.

Antoine Watteau

Valenciennes, 1684
Nogent sur Marne, 1721

Studies of Figures

Red chalk on cream paper
9.2 x 13.2
Léonce Mesnard bequest, 1890

Gabriel-François Doyen

Paris, 1726
Saint Petersburg (Russia), 1806

The Martyrdom of Saint Sebastian

Pen and brown ink, brown wash,
white gouache highlights on blue paper
44.2 x 35.3
Source unknown

Jacques-Louis David

Paris, 1726
Brussels (Belgium), 1825

Frieze in the Antique Style

1780
Pen and black ink, grey wash, white
gouache highlights on browned blue paper
26.8 x 74.6
Aristide Rey Bequest, 1931

214 The 19th Century

Three quarters of the 1,700 drawings in the 19th century collection have now been classified. Great efforts have been made to preserve these works, which are often more delicate than older drawings. For this period, there are large groups of the works of individual artists, and especially Delacroix, whose work, as represented in the museum, includes landscapes, studies of Moroccan figures, and various preliminary studies, among which are *Jacob Fighting with the Angel* and the *Study for Drapery* shown here (and which was used by the painter for the *Virgin of the Sacred Heart*, now in the cathedral of Ajaccio). This work, dating from Delacroix's early period, is a real technical demonstration, and contrasts with the pen drawings, which herald Matisse's work.

The mixture of everyday realism and enigmatic poetry peculiar to Jean-François Millet gives great power, despite its small format, to *The Horse Ride*. Rigid lines make the figures stand out against a roughly sketched landscape suggesting the harmony between man and nature that was dear to the hearts of the Barbizon painters.

In contrast to this simplicity, Gustave Doré's landscapes are imposing and magnificent, whether on paper or on canvas. There are a few startling examples in the Grenoble collection: *Mountain Stream among Pines*, a large watercolour where the artist's feeling for mountains, for their mystery and power, are as perfectly illustrated as in his famous painting, *Scottish Lake after a Storm*, which is also owned by the museum.

Eugène Delacroix

Charenton, 1798
Paris, 1863

Study for Drapery

Charcoal and white chalk on beige paper
56.7 x 41.8
Source unknown

Jean-François Millet

Gruchy, 1814
Barbizon, 1875

The Horse Ride

Black chalk on cream paper
11.9 x 19.4
Léonce Mesnard bequest, 1890

Gustave Doré

Strasbourg, 1832
Paris, 1883

Mountain Stream among Pines

Watercolour on paper
49 x 33.6
Aristide Rey Bequest, 1931

The End of the 19th Century

Some of the forerunners of modern art, close to the Impressionists, were accomplished draughtsmen. This is the case for two artists who had strong links with the Grenoble region, and whose work is well represented in the museum.

Johann Bartold Jongkind, who spent the last years of his life in the Dauphiné, was so fond of its landscapes that he renewed his entire technique in order to study and paint them. The innumerable watercolour landscapes he produced, from Grenoble itself to la Côte Saint André (his adoptive town), became more and more spontaneous, free, and full of virtuosity. Jongkind often left most of the paper untouched, reducing the colour to a few splashes in order to render, as if by magic, the finest nuances of the atmosphere.

Fantin-Latour, though he did not end his life in the Dauphiné, was born in Grenoble. Thanks to the bequest of Mme Fantin-Latour in 1921, 150 drawings and a series of lithographs complement the famous group of paintings held by the Museum of Grenoble. Every aspect of the work of this artist, who formed a link between the academic tradition and the most advanced tendencies of his time, are represented in the collection: compositions inspired by literary and musical subjects, studies of models and portraits. In his 1861 *Self-portrait*, charcoal deepens the shaded area, which was often used by Fantin-Latour to set off his figures.

With Gauguin and his study for the painting *Te nave Nave Fenua*, which is now now at the Ohara Museum in Japan, we have the absolute antithesis of Fantin-Latour: the colour, applied flat or in dots, is its own expressive power; the *Tahitian Eve* is filled with this strength, and moves us, to use the artist's own words, with "something penetrating, mysterious, at the edge of the infinite."

Henri Fantin-Latour

Grenoble, 1836
Buré, 1904

Self-portrait

1861
Charcoal on beige paper
39.2 x 32.4
Gift of Mme Henri Fantin-Latour, 1904

Johann Bartold Jongkind

Lattrop, 1819
La Côte Saint André, 1891

View of Grenoble

Watercolour on cream paper
17.3 x 50.8
Acquired in 1893

Paul Gauguin

Paris, 1848
Atuana (Marquesas Islands), 1903

Tahitian Eve

1892
Pen and India ink, watercolour and gouache on beige paper
29.9 x 21.3
Agutte-Sembat Bequest, 1923

Modern Drawings

Among the museum's drawings and prints there is a remarkable, and comprehensive, collection of 20th century works, through which — and this is rare in France — it is possible to follow the history of the art of this century, and indeed that of modern art as such.

The collection was put together largely from gifts made by artists or their families, as well as by collectors. Its presentation will be regularly renewed, so as to enable visitors to discover, and study, these works.

The Acrobat

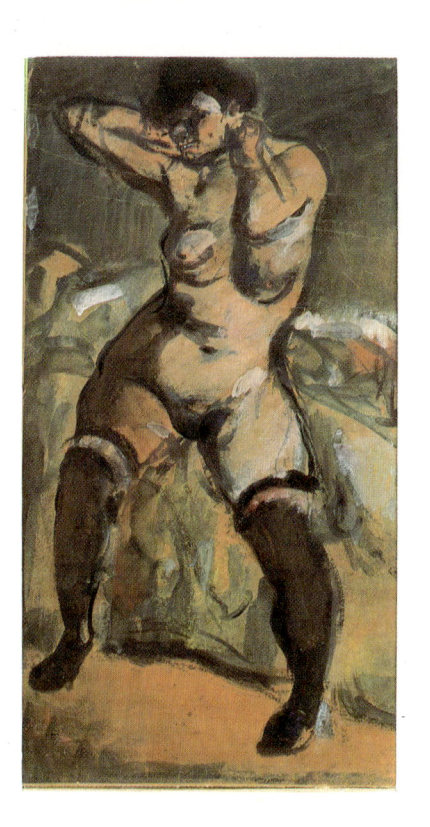

1906
Gouache and watercolour on paper,
mounted on cardboard
41 x 23
Agutte-Sembat Bequest, 1923

Georges Rouault

Paris, 1871-1958

The Acrobat illustrates Rouault's realistic vision of destitute, downtrodden humanity, as depicted in the works he produced between 1903 and 1906. The dark tones of the flesh, the contrasted light, the exaggerated character of the pose and the broad brushstrokes, lend this watercolour an atmosphere of violence, and express the tragic intensity of the model. During the period in question, Rouault's works were peopled with terrible images of prostitutes and clowns, the witnesses of his desperate approach to human reality, the direct opposite of the gay, colourful vision of the Fauvist painters.

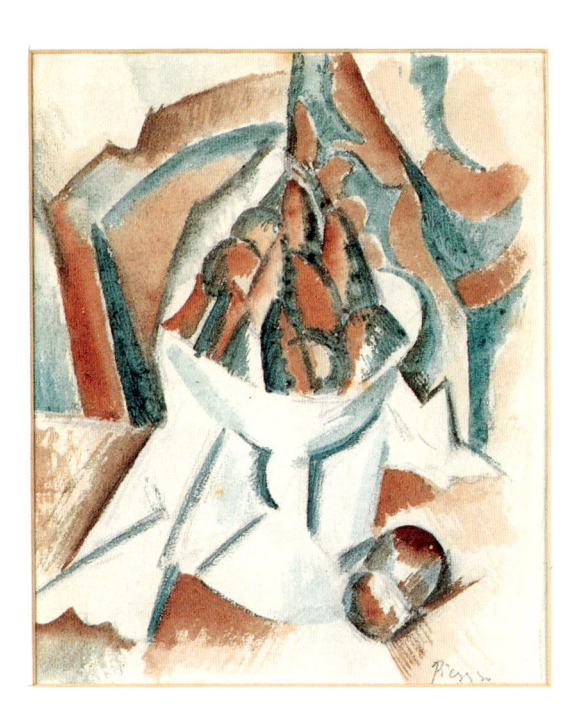

Pablo Picasso

(Pablo Ruiz y Picasso)

Málaga (Spain), 1881
Mougins, 1973

The Fruit Bowl

1909
Pencil and watercolour on paper
27 x 23
Acquired in 1934

This drawing belongs to the period, between 1907 and 1909, known as "Cubisme Cézannien". Between the summer of 1908 and the winter of 1909, Picasso produced a great number of still lifes, and here the volumes of the objects on the table — the fruit bowl and the fruit it contains — are broken up into planes and reduced to facets which cancel all effects of perspective. The volume of each object is, so to speak, exploded so as to enable the viewer to see every side of the still life, which is described from various viewpoints and tends to become one with the plane of the drawing. The dark colours, mainly greens and dark browns, were borrowed from Cézanne, and are characteristic of Picasso's first Cubist period.

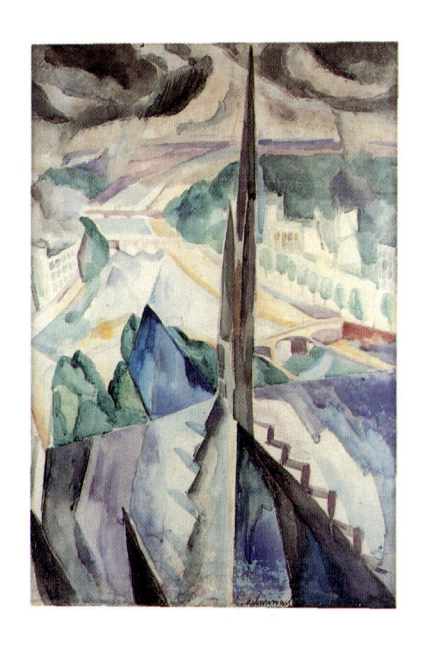

The Steeple of Notre Dame

1909
Watercolour on paper, mounted on canvas
65 x 46
Acquired in 1947

Robert Delaunay

Paris, 1885
Montpellier, 1941

Robert Delaunay's version of Cubism, as is obvious in this watercolour, was highly original: through the use of light, which transforms the subject, the artist breaks up the form, and describes it as a set of coloured facets. The image — in this case the nave, the central steeple and the aisles of Notre Dame — does not obey the laws of perspective, but is made to fly apart into distinct and juxtaposed fragments that give the subject and the various parts of the composition a certain independence and mobility. Images of Paris and its monuments are very frequent in the work of Delaunay, especially between 1909 and 1918, and gave rise to some of his most famous paintings. His favourite themes were turned into series: Notre Dame cathedral and the church of Saint Séverin are the two religious monuments most often illustrated in his work.

Henri Matisse

La Danse

Le Cateau Cambrésis, 1869
Nice, 1954

1909-1910
Charcoal on paper
48 x 65
Agutte-Sembat Bequest, 1923

This sketch for *La Danse* is one of Matisse's most successful studies for the decoration project commissioned by Shchukin, the celebrated Russian collector, for the staircase of his Troubetskoy town-house. In March 1909, he commissioned Matisse to do a first panel, illustrating *La Danse*, which was followed by a second panel, *La Musique*. The first version of *La Danse*, now at Museum of Modern Art in New York, was painted in just one or two days at the beginning of 1909; Matisse spent more time on the Grenoble sketch, which was executed afterwards and was more successful than the New York painting. It reveals Matisse's technique as a draughtsman; the experimentation, erasures, and corrections, as well as the multiple lines, perfectly express the curves of the moving bodies. The naked dancers, drawn as a garland of flexible arabesques, illustrate the circular movement of the dance. *La Danse* and *La Musique* were exhibited at the 1910 Salon d'Automne before being sent to Moscow, where they were installed the same year; they are now in the Hermitage Museum.

Woman with a Blue Tunic

1914
Gouache on paper, mounted on cardboard
65 x 51
Agutte-Sembat Bequest, 1923

Édouard Vuillard

Cuiseaux, 1868
La Baule, 1940

This gouache, painted in such a way that it might easily be mistaken for an oil painting, was executed after the artist's Nabi period; the subject, the atmosphere and the matt aspect still belong, however, to that period. A woman is shown sitting on a sofa in the corner of a studio. The composition, based on a few diagonals, is extremely simple; the artist is essentially interested in the relations between colours and the treatment of surfaces, especially the translation of the light, which softly emphasizes the forms. The blue pigment of the blouse is emphasized by the colours surrounding it. There is no noise, no movement, to disturb the tranquillity so often found in Vuillard's compositions.

Juan Gris

Madrid (Spain), 1887
Boulogne sur Mer, 1927

Bottle, Glass and Pipe

1917
Lead pencil on paper
33.5 x 27.5
Acquired in 1971

This drawing, a still life dated 1917, announces Juan Gris' "synthetic" period, which was characterized by the sobriety of his Cubist language, and during which he produced some of his best paintings, such as *Bottle, Glass and Pipe*, whose composition is based on a sophisticated arrangement of forms in a frontal space: the glass, the bottle, the pipe, the newspaper and the frame are placed on a table whose veined surface is reminiscent of works produced by the collage technique. Faithful to Cubist experimentation — the dislocation and fragmentation of objects — Juan Gris, by painting the subject from above, by reversing the planes, by taking different viewpoints, uncovers the structural characteristics of the object. A cylinder becomes a bottle or a glass, a white rectangle a newspaper, a right angle a frame; and the objects are revealed by the contrasts of light and shade.

There is also, in the museum's collection, a gouache dating from 1922, *Still Life with a Bottle*, dedicated to the celebrated German art critic Carl Einstein.

Invention

1918
Lead pencil and watercolour on paper
43 x 34
Acquired in 1949

Fernand Léger

Argentan, 1881
Gif sur Yvette, 1955

Invention is a highly successful study for the painting *In the Factory (Pattern for the Engine)*, dating from the same year. After the First World War, Fernand Léger became enthusiastic about industrial civilization and the modern world; he eulogized them, and exalted the poetry of the machine. In the watercolour shown here, the figurative elements are totally dislocated, and the vision of the factory is translated into entanglements of cones, planes, tubes, cylinders and geometrical shapes that introduce a dynamic tension. Léger searched for plastic equivalents to objects and machines, transcribing the syncopated rhythm of the modern world. His approach, which attempts to express the life and animated environment of the factory through fragmentation, and through the juxtaposition of planes with precisely-drawn edges, has a lot in common with abstraction.

Amedeo Modigliani

Livorno (Italy), 1884
Paris, 1920

Portrait of Paul Dermée

1919
Lead pencil on paper
33 x 25
Acquired in 1937

This portrait of the poet Paul Dermée — who founded, in 1917, the magazine *Nord-Sud*, and, in 1921 (with Ozenfant and Le Corbusier), *L'Esprit Nouveau* — can be dated 1919. It is characteristic of the style of Modigliani, whose art was on the fringes of Cubism, and shows his talent as a portraitist. By its stylization of form, its accentuation of line and its elimination of detail, this figure is imbued with great expressiveness. The arabesque used by Modigliani to enclose the shape enables him to indicate volume without having to resort to values. The two tones that are to be seen on the paper are due to its prolonged exposition to the light in a mount that was smaller than the surface of the paper. There are four other drawings by Modigliani in the Museum of Grenoble.

Roger de La Fresnaye

Le Mans, 1885
Grasse, 1925

The Drum

1919
Watercolour on paper
27 x 21
Acquired in 1928

The Drum is one of the last works produced by Roger de La Fresnaye in Cubist spirit. The presence of objects is conveyed through geometrical shapes — squares, rectangles, circles and curves — done with lines or in flat areas of colour. The letters, reminiscent of the stencil technique, are similar to those used by Picasso and Braque. This composition, which, in its effects, is very close to a collage, finds a rhythm in the contrasts between shapes, and is almost an abstract work.

The Chinese Nightingale

1920
Collage
12.2 x 8.8
Gift of the Genon-Catalot family, 1992

Max Ernst

Brühl (Germany), 1891
Paris, 1976

It was thanks to the generosity of the Genon-Catalot family that this collage, dated 1920, became part of the collections of the museum in 1992. It was in 1920 that Max Ernst went to Paris, where he produced a number of collages in the Dadaist spirit; these resemble works created at the same time by the Berlin artists Raoul Hausmann, John Heartfield and Hannah Höch. *The Chinese Nightingale*, like the other collages done by the artist around the same time, is composed of photographs clipped from mail-order catalogues and technical encyclopædias. The objects put together here, a bomb and bomb rack, are an evocation of war and destruction. However, with the association of the fan, the scarf and the graceful movement of the arms, the work takes on an unreal, poetic character specific to Max Ernst's Dadaism, strongly contrasting with the social critique of the Berlin artists. The artist made five photographic enlargements of this original collage.

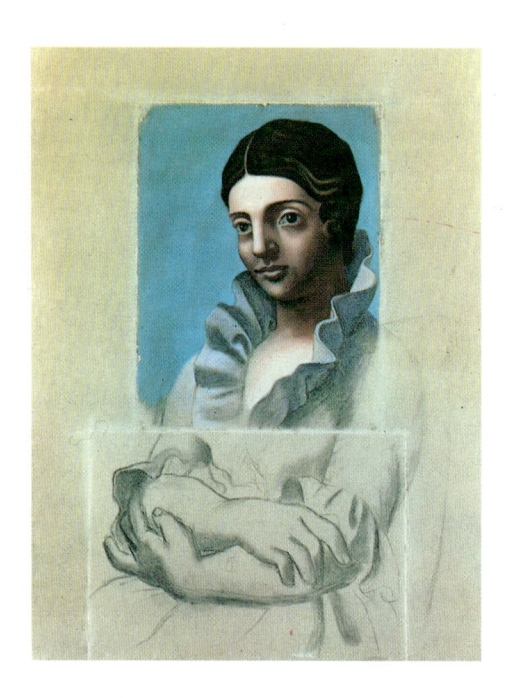

Pablo Picasso

(Pablo Ruiz y Picasso)

Málaga (Spain), 1881
Mougins, 1973

Portrait of Olga

1921
Pastel and charcoal on paper,
mounted on canvas
127 x 96.5
Loaned by the Musée National d'Art
Moderne (Picasso Donation), 1991

Picasso produced numerous portraits of his wife, Olga Kokhlova, a dancer with the Ballets Russes whom he met in Rome in 1917 while working on the stage sets for the ballet *Parade*. The upper part of the model was meticulously drawn in pastel on a vertical sheet of paper, below which there is a charcoal sketch of the waist and hands, executed on a separate sheet of paper of horizontal format. The two sheets were then mounted on a larger support, and the figure was completed by a few rough lines. The striking aspect of this assemblage is due to the different treatment of the face, depicted in colour with a strong shading to indicate volume, from that of the rest of the body — a few lines with a light shading. This portrait, which belongs to Picasso's "Neoclassical" period, with its massive, sculptural forms inspired by the art of Antiquity, has a compelling presence. The face, with its simple, regular features, is crowned by a weighty hairstyle and framed in the heavy folds of a ruff. The stylization of forms, their anonymous character and the absence of any psychological depth, contribute to the monumental quality of the figure.

Child with Balloon

1925
Pastel on paper
75 x 43
Acquired in 1926

Maria Blanchard

Santander (Spain), 1881
Paris, 1932

While living in Spain, between 1913 and 1916, Maria Blanchard met Lipchitz and Diego Rivera, who, on her return to France, introduced her to Pablo Picasso and Juan Gris. They initiated her into Cubism, and her subsequent work was particularly influenced by Gris. After a little-noted Cubist period, Blanchard painted in the fairly heavy figurative style, full of tenderness, that can be seen in *Child with Balloon*. The dull, melting colours, the volume given to the forms, and the clarity of the composition of this pastel, are signs of her return to Classicism, and to a more traditional representation of the subject. The geometrical asceticism, close to the art of Gris, can be seen in the somewhat dry treatment of perspective and in the volume of the figures.

Marc Chagall

Vitebsk (Bielorussia), 1887
Saint Paul de Vence, 1985

The Church

1926
Lead pencil and gouache on paper,
mounted on cardboard
67 x 52
Acquired in 1928

The Church was painted during Chagall's second French period, between 1923 and 1941, when Ambroise Vollard commissioned him to illustrate Gogol's *Dead Souls*, La Fontaine's *Fables* and the Bible. He made a few trips to the country during that time, particularly to the village of Chambron sur Lac, in the Puy de Dôme, in 1926, where he painted the church shown here. This building appears in several of Chagall's paintings; here it is the exclusive subject. The drawing and the technique are naïve, almost childish, in the description of the religious edifice, the landscape and the sky behind the steeple. These elements are evidence of the joyful, truculent vigour of this original, unclassifiable artist, whose work is always full of poetry and a feeling of wonder.

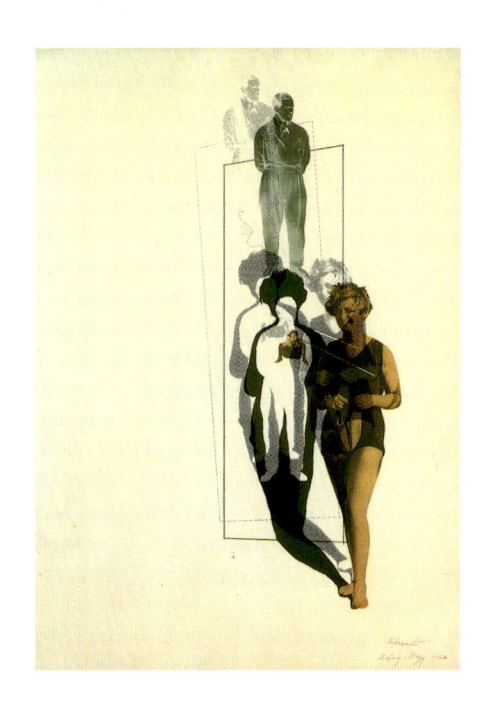

Eifersucht

1927
Photomontage and India ink pen drawing
63 x 45
Acquired in 1971

László Moholy-Nagy

Borsod (Hungary), 1895
Chicago, Illinois, 1946

Moholy-Nagy expressed his art, which was based on a rigorous experimental practice, in the most varied domains: painting, sculpture, typography, photography, collage, photomontage, stage sets; he also taught at the Bauhaus, in Weimar, from 1923 to 1928, and later at the Art Institute of Chicago. Between 1924 and 1927, he produced a series of photomontages, of which *Eifersucht* (Jealousy) is a typical example. This composition (a similar picture exists at the Victoria and Albert Museum in London), is made of cut-out photographs mounted on a background, with details added in India ink. The figure of a swimmer in the foreground is dominated by a negative photograph of Moholy-Nagy in an engineer's boiler suit. The shadow of the woman in a bathing costume is drawn on the ground and continues on a vertical panel which resembles a target for shooting practice. The blank silhouette of Moholy-Nagy also appears there, and inside it, the crouching figure of a woman aiming with a gun at the heart of the swimmer. With its asymmetrical layout, and the subtle relationship between the collage and the drawn elements, this allegorical photomontage is a clear evocation of the "new vision" Moholy-Nagy was searching for, and which, in the present case, is curiously reminiscent of the art of Giorgio De Chirico and Carlo Carrà.

Joan Miró

Barcelona (Spain), 1893
Palma (Spain), 1983

Figure with White Rectangle

1928
Gouache and charcoal on paper
106 x 73
Gift of Pierre Loeb, 1928

Miró elaborated his poetical, fantastical universe as a result of his contact with the Surrealist painters and writers in Paris. His Surrealist period took shape between 1925 and 1927, when he invented and evoked a symbolic, magical world. *Figure with White Rectangle* represents, on an unevenly covered ochre background, a roughly drawn line figure. This totally unrealistic form, placed on a flat surface, has been given an immense eye in white gouache, and a ridiculous nose; the rest of the body, barely sketched, is adorned with two black rectangles which touch at one corner, and also by a large white surface, while an enigmatic number 5 is spread out over the lower part of the composition. Half-way between abstraction and poetic evocation, this drawing reveals the originality of Miró's art among the Surrealists.

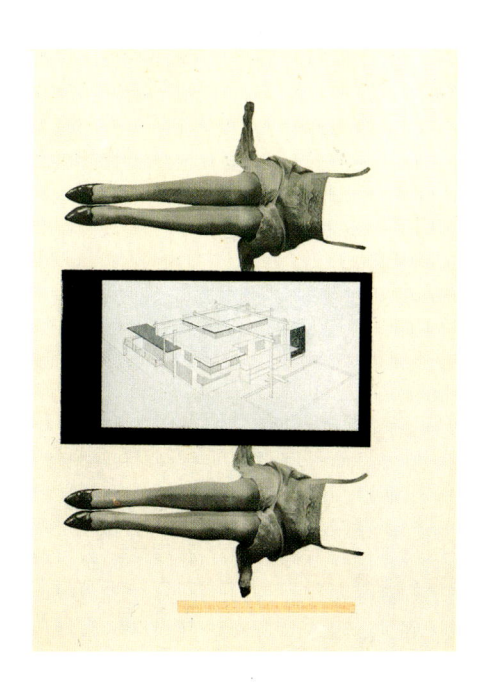

Composition N° 48

1928
Photomontage
35.5 x 26
Acquired in 1987

Friedrich Vordemberge-Gildewart

Osnabrück (Germany), 1899
Ulm (Germany), 1962

Friedrich Vordemberge-Gildewart, after studying architecture and sculpture in Hanover, became a member of the Sturm group in Berlin, and participated in the De Stijl movement from 1924 on. *Composition N° 48* shows his interest in Neoclassicism and the technique of Dadaist photomontage as it was applied by Hannah Hoch, Raoul Hausmann and John Heartfield. This composition, featuring the photograph of an architectural project for a country house (designed, in 1923, by the artist), is surrounded by a black frame, and by two identical photographs, each showing a pair of female legs emerging from a luxurious slip; these photographs are placed in parallel above and below that of the architectural project. The title of the work, typed on a paper strip, reinforces the mysterious meaning of the composition: "architektur... keine optische wertung" (architecture... no optical classification). The museum has another photomontage dating from 1928, as well as a drawing, and a collage from 1947.

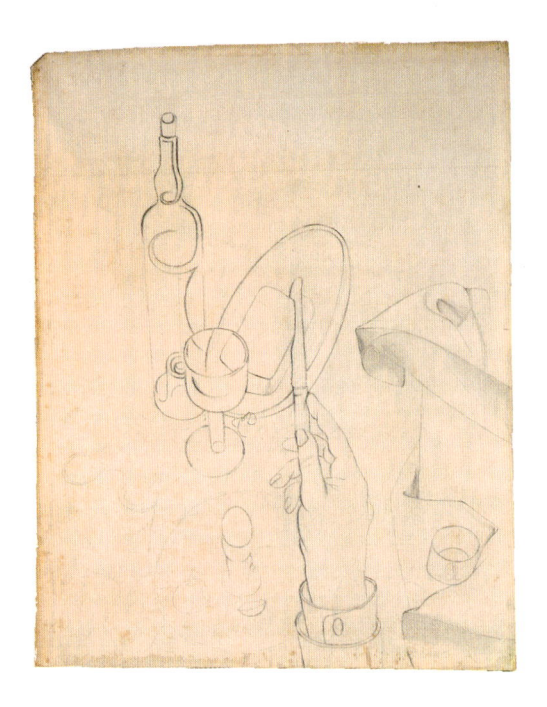

Amédée Ozenfant

Saint Quentin, 1886
Cannes, 1966

The Artist's Hand

1929
Lead pencil on paper
70 x 56
Acquired in 1971

This drawing was no doubt a preliminary study for *The Bachelor* (Paris, private collection), probably painted in 1930. The vision is subjective, and the hand which enters the composition from the bottom is that of the artist. The composition, which is original, seen from above, features a tiered arrangement of shapes. The objects — the bottle, the glass, the egg-cup and egg, the serviette ring, etc. — are drawn with great precision using a technique close to the principles of Purism, and resembles axonometric projections and industrial drawings. Hands were at that time a recurrent theme in Ozenfant's work. In this particular drawing, whose precision of line recalls Ingres, Ozenfant expresses volumes without the use of shading.

Seated Nude

1931
Charcoal on paper
102 x 68
Acquired in 1934

Aristide Maillol

Banyuls sur Mer, 1861
Perpignan, 1944

Maillol was a Nabi painter before becoming one of the greatest sculptors of the 20th century. He also produced and published fine books, for which he made the paper himself from pure rags; this drawing was made on such paper. The female nude, his favourite theme in sculpture, is a pretext for the construction of an extremely simple form, with a dense volume and tense lines. The classical drapery around the model's legs and her meditative expression are reminiscent of the art of Puvis de Chavannes. The lack of expression in the face, and the stylization of the forms, give this drawing the same timeless aspect as Maillol's sculpted figures.

Willi Baumeister

Stuttgart (Germany), 1889-1955

The Painter

1931-1932
Lead pencil and charcoal on paper
35.5 x 26.2
Gift of the artist, 1933

The Museum of Grenoble has ten drawings by Willi Baumeister; this one features the theme of the painter and his model. The figures and the palette are depicted by means of stylized, almost geometrical forms, reminiscent of industrial drawing and the stark blueprints of machines. Here, Baumeister's art can be related to that of Fernand Léger — who could be said to have been his equivalent in France — and to the principles enunciated by Le Corbusier and Ozenfant in their Purist works.

The Spread-out Figures

1938
Pencil on paper
32 x 23.5
Acquired in 1973

Sophie Taeuber-Arp

Davos (Switzerland), 1889
Zurich (Switzerland), 1943

Sophie Taeuber-Arp participated, with her husband Jean Arp, in the foundation of the Dadaist movement in Zurich in 1916. Over the course of her life, she worked in a great variety of modes of expression: painting, sculpture, relief, architecture, puppets and choreography. This 1938 drawing, which can be compared with the painting *Graduated Sequence* (also in the museum), clearly shows the method used by the artist; with a number of similar shapes, and playing with changes in proportion and space, she reveals various movements and tensions. Four similar figures, one of them back to front, are made up of two more or less identical shapes combining curves and straight lines. Their relations create a composition expressing rhythm. The space occupied by the figures in the composition, and the movement they suggest, speak of gracious, light dance steps.

Kurt Schwitters

Hanover (Germany), 1887
Ambleside (Great Britain), 1948

De Stijl 47-14

1947
Collage
27.5 x 22.2
Acquired in 1926

In 1918, Schwitters abandoned the traditional techniques of painting, and introduced, in works he called *Merzbilder*, residues of everyday life: tram tickets, paper torn from posters, tin cans, various advertisements, wrapping paper, old rags, bits of strings and other odd objects. This humble material, transformed into works of art, was meant to be used for the construction of a new world. *De Stijl 47-14* illustrates the links he maintained, from 1923 on, with the Dutch movement De Stijl, and especially with Théo Van Doesburg. This collage was executed not long before the death of the artist, with bits torn out of the magazine *De Stijl*, along with various pieces of paper and some stamps: it clearly indicates Schwitters' debt to Constructivism and to the community of minds that linked him with the artists of that movement. The pieces of paper are placed according to their shape and colour, and give rise to a rigorous composition which can be seen as a nostalgic homage to Constructivism.

Selective Bibliography

Germain Viatte, *Dessins modernes*
Inventaire des collections publiques françaises, tome 8
Réunion des musées nationaux, Paris, 1963.

Gabrielle Kueny et Jean Yoyotte
Grenoble, musée des Beaux-Arts, collection égyptienne
Inventaire des collections publiques françaises, tome 24
Réunion des musées nationaux, Paris, 1979.

Hélène Vincent
*Andry-Farcy, un conservateur novateur
Le Musée de Grenoble de 1919 à 1949,* Musée de Grenoble, 1982.

Serge Lemoine, *Le Musée de Grenoble*
Monuments et Musées de France, Fondation Paribas, Paris, 1988.

Marco Chiarini, *Tableaux italiens*
Musée de Grenoble, 1988.

Chefs-d'œuvre du Musée de Grenoble, de David à Picasso
Fondation de l'Hermitage, Lausanne, 1992-1993.

Catherine Chevillot
Peinture et sculpture du XIXe siècle, la collection du musée de Grenoble
Réunion des musées nationaux, Paris, 1994.

Gilles Chomer
Peinture française, la collection du musée de Grenoble
Réunion des musées nationaux, Paris, 1994.

Marcel Destot
Peinture des écoles du nord, la collection du musée de Grenoble
Réunion des musées nationaux, Paris, 1994.

Serge Lemoine, editor
L'art du XXe siècle, la collection du musée de Grenoble
Réunion des musées nationaux, Paris, 1994.

Serge Lemoine, *Le Musée de Grenoble*
Beaux-Arts Magazine, numéro spécial hors-série, Paris, 1994.

Jean Rosen et Dominique Forest
Faïences, la collection du musée de Grenoble
Réunion des musées nationaux, Paris, 1994.

**Index of works reproduced,
by artist's names** 241

Bold characters indicate page number

Achard, Jean, **87**
L'Albane, (Francesco Albani), **34**
Agutte, Georgette, **99**
Andre, Carl, **187**
Antiquities, **14**, **15**, **16**
Arp, Jean, **136**

Baciccio, (Giovanni Battista Gaulli), **205**
Balthus,
(Balthazar Klossowski de Rola), **152**
Bartholdi, Frédéric-Auguste, **85**
Bartolo, Taddeo di, **20**
Bauchant, André, **156**
Baumeister, Willi, **236**
Beert, Osias, **36**
Béöthy, Étienne, **142**
Berghe, Frits van den, **154**
Bertier, Charles, **89**
Blanchard, Maria, **229**
Bloemaert, Abraham, **32**
Boltanski, Christian, **200**
Bonnard, Pierre, **128**
Boucher de Bourges,
(Jean Boucher), **211**
Boudin, Eugène, **92**
Boullogne the Younger,
Louis de, **211**
Braque, Georges, **109**
Breenbergh, Bartholomeus, **39**, **209**
Brenet, Nicolas-Guy, **66**
Bury, Pol, **169**

Cahn, Marcelle, **122**
Calder, Alexander, **162**
Camoin, Charles, **105**
Canaletto,
(Giovanni Antonio Canal), **71**
Carracci, Annibale, **33**
Cerquozzi, Michelangelo, **35**
Chagall, Marc, **114**, **230**
Champaigne, Philippe de, **51**, **52**, **53**
Cornell, Joseph, **149**
Cragg, Tony, **196**
Crayer, Caspar de, **27**

David, Jacques-Louis, **75**, **213**
De Chirico, Giorgio, **124**, **125**
De Pisis, Filippo, **147**
De Smet, Gustave, **155**
Debré, Olivier, **175**
Delacroix, Eugène, **79**, **215**
Delaunay, Robert, **110**, **221**
Derain, André, **103**, **115**
Desportes, François, **64**
Domela, César, **133**

Domenichino
(Domenico Zampieri), **31**
Doré, Gustave, **83**, **215**
Doyen, Gabriel-François, **213**
Dubuffet, Jean, **176**
Duchamp-Villon, Raymond, **111**
Durameau, Louis-Jean-Jacques, **65**

Eliasz, Nicolaes, "Pickenoy", **45**
Ernst, Max, **145**, **227**
Étienne-Martin, **177**

Fantin-Latour, Henri, **91**, **217**
Fautrier, Jean, **158**
Federle, Helmut, **198**
Flandrin, Jules, **129**
Foschi, Francesco, **73**
Francis, Sam, **182**
Friesz, Émile Othon, **108**

Gabo, Naum, **141**
Gauguin, Paul, **95**, **217**
Giacometti, Alberto, **151**
Gilbert and George, **193**
Gilioli, Émile, **165**
Girodet, (Anne-Louis Girodet
de Roucy-Trioson), **76**
Gleizes, Albert, **117**
Gonzalez, Julio, **159**
Gorin, Jean, **143**
Graeser, Camille, **160**
Gris, Juan, **224**
Gromaire, Marcel, **123**
Grosz, George, **153**
Guardi, Francesco, **72**
Guétal, Laurent, **88**

Hajdu, Étienne, **173**
Hartung, Hans, **171**
Hébert, Ernest, **86**
Hélion, Jean, **134**
Herbin, Auguste, **137**
Honegger, Gottfried, **167**
Horn, Rebecca, **195**
Houdon, Jean-Antoine, **68**

Ingres, Jean-Auguste-Dominique, **77**

Jongkind, Johann Bartold, **217**
Jordaens, Jacob, **30**, **209**
Jouvenet, Jean-Baptiste, **57**
Judd, Donald, **188**

Klee, Paul, **144**
Kounellis, Jannis, **194**

La Fresnaye, Roger de, **226**
La Hyre, Laurent de, **54**
La Tour, Georges de, **47**
Laemlein, Alexandre, **82**
Lardera, Berto, **164**
Largillière, Nicolas de, **62**
Laurens, Henri, **113**
Lavier, Bertrand, **201**
Le Brun, Charles (school of), **56**
Le Sueur, Eustache, **55**
Léger, Fernand, **120**, **121**, **225**
LeWitt, Sol, **186**
Lhose, Richard Paul, **161**
Lombard School, **205**
Lorrain, Claude (C. Gellée), **48**

Magnelli, Alberto, **116**
Magritte, René, **146**
Maillol, Aristide, **235**
Mangold, Robert, **185**
Marden, Brice, **184**
Marquet, Albert, **104**
Matisse, Henri, **100**, **101**, **102**, **222**
Mauzaisse, Jean-Baptiste, **81**
McCollum, Allan, **197**
Messager, Annette, **199**
Millet, Jean-François, **215**
Miró, Joan, **232**
Modigliani, Amedeo, **226**
Moholy-Nagy, Laszlo, **231**
Monet, Claude, **94**
Monory, Jacques, **180**
Morellet, François, **168**

Nevelson, Louise, **181**

Ozenfant, Amédée, **119**, **234**

Palma Giovane, Jacopo, **207**
Pannini, Giovanni Paolo, **70**
Parmentier, Michel, **192**
Parmigianino,
(Francesco Mazzola), **205**
Pascin, Jules, **130**
Pasmore, Victor, **166**
Il Perugino, (Pietro Vannuci), **21**
Peyrissac, Jean, **138**
Picabia, Francis, **157**
Picasso, Pablo, **118**, **220**, **228**
Pradier, James, **84**
Preti, Mattia, **26**
Prinner, Anton, **140**

Raysse, Martial, **179**
Restout, Jean, **63**

Ricci, Sebastiano, **69**
Rouault, Georges, **219**
Rubens, Peter Paul, **29**
Russolo, Luigi, **112**

Scheffer, Ary, **80**
Schwitters, Kurt, **238**
Sermézy, Clémence Sophie de, **78**
Sesto, Cesare da, **22**
Signac, Paul, **98**
Sisley, Alfred, **93**
Smith, Leon Polk, **183**
Snyders, Frans, **38**
Soulages, Pierre, **170**
Soutine, Chaïm, **127**
Staël, Nicolas de, **174**
Stomer, Matthias, **42**
Strobel, Bartholomäus, **43**
Strozzi, Bernardo, **25**

Tanguy, Yves, **148**
Taeuber-Arp, Sophie, **135**, **237**
Téniers, David, **37**
Tiepolo, Giambattista, **207**
Toroni, Niele, **191**
Torres-Garcia, Joaquin, **139**
Torriti, Jacopo, **19**

Vallotton, Félix, **96**
Van den Eeckhout, Gerbrand, **44**
Van der Leck, Bart, **132**
Van Doesburg, Théo, **131**
Van Dongen, Kees, **106**
Van Ruysdael, Salomon, **41**
Van Saftleven, Herman, **209**
Van Swanevelt, Herman, **40**
Vasarely, Victor, **163**
Vasari, Giorgio, **24**
Venet, Bernar, **189**
Veronese, (Paolo Caliari), **23**, **207**
Viallat, Claude, **190**
Victor Brauner, **150**
Vieira da Silva, Maria-Elena, **172**
Vien, Joseph-Marie, **67**
Vignon, Claude, **46**
Vlaminck, Maurice de, **107**
Vordemberge-Gildewart, Friedrich, **233**
Vouet, Simon, **49**, **211**
Vuillard, Édouard, **223**

Watteau, Antoine, **213**
Wesselman, Tom, **178**

Zadkine, Ossip, **126**
Zurbarán, Francesco de, **58**, **60**

PHOTOGRAPHIC CREDITS
Jean-Francois Lucas and André Morin.
All rights reserved.

From the publications department,
directed by Anne de Margerie

EDITORIAL COORDINATION
Gilles Fage, Rmn, Lyon,
with the collaboration
of Dominique Royer

FABRICATION
Jacques Venelli

GRAPHIC DESIGN AND LAYOUT
Jean-Yves Cousseau
assisted by Sarah Clément

This work was printed in September 1994 on
Royal Satin 135-g paper, on the presses of
the Laffont printing house in Avignon.

PHOTO-ENGRAVING
TEI, Villeurbanne

BINDING
Façonnage Alain, Saint-Marcel-les-Annonay

FLASHING
temps réel, Dijon

Dépôt légal : septembre 1994
ISBN 2 7118 3149 3
GK 39 3149